BEST NEWSPAPER WRITING
1993

WINNERS: THE AMERICAN SOCIETY OF NEWSPAPER EDITORS COMPETITION

EDITED BY DON FRY

97 96 95 94 93   5 4 3 2 1

Library of Congress Catalog Card Number: 93-72145

International Standard Book Number: 1–56625–029–3

The Poynter Institute for Media Studies
801 Third Street South
St. Petersburg, Florida 33701

Bonus Books, Inc.
160 East Illinois Street
Chicago, Illinois 60611

Printed in the United States of America

Fifteen years of interviewing the winners of this prize tells us that no writer wins it alone. So we dedicate this volume to editors, copy editors, photographers, artists, and designers, to all the members of newsroom teams who serve our readers.

About this series

JUNE 1993

The Poynter Institute for Media Studies proudly publishes the 15th volume of its series *Best Newspaper Writing,* valued since 1979 by students, teachers, and professionals as an indispensable text on clear, effective, and graceful newswriting.

As in past years, *Best Newspaper Writing* is a joint venture of the Institute and the American Society of Newspaper Editors (ASNE). In 1978, ASNE made the improvement of newspaper writing one of its primary goals. The Society inaugurated a contest to select the best writing from newspapers in the United States and Canada, and to reward the winning writers with $2,500 prizes. The Institute volunteered to spread the gospel of good writing by publishing the winning entries along with notes, commentaries, and interviews. That first volume, *Best Newspaper Writing 1979,* sold out long ago and has become a collector's item.

Dr. Don Fry, an associate of the Institute and current director of Poynter writing programs, resumes editorship of *Best Newspaper Writing* this year. Fry took over the series in 1986 from Dr. Roy Peter Clark, who edited the first six editions. In 1990, Fry was joined as co-editor by Poynter colleague Dr. Karen F. Brown, who edited the book in 1991 and 1992.

The 1993 award categories are non-deadline writing, deadline writing, commentary, editorial writing, and headline writing. A committee of 15 editors, chaired by Louis D. Boccardi, president and chief executive officer of the Associated Press, judged this year's entries:

> Larry Allison, *Long Beach* (Calif.) *Press-Telegram*
>
> N. Christian Anderson, *The Register,* Orange County, Calif.

Judith Brown, *New Britain* (Conn.) *Herald*
Judith Clabes, *The Kentucky Post*
Jack Fuller, *Chicago Tribune*
Robert Giles, *The Detroit News*
Jane Healy, *The Orlando* (Fla.) *Sentinel*
Deborah Howell, Newhouse News Service, Washington, D.C.
David Lawrence, *The Miami Herald*
Tony Marro, *Newsday,* Long Island, N.Y.
Susan Miller, Scripps Howard, Cincinnati
Acel Moore, *The Philadelphia Inquirer*
Ted Natt, *The Daily News,* Longview, Wash.
Burl Osborne, *Dallas Morning News*

The Institute congratulates the winners and finalists of the ASNE Distinguished Writing Awards, and thanks the judges for their fine work and dedication to good writing.

* * *

Founded in 1975 by the late Nelson Poynter, chairman of the *St. Petersburg Times* and its Washington affiliate, *Congressional Quarterly,* the Institute was bequeathed Poynter's controlling stock in the Times Publishing Company in 1978. It invests its dividends in educational activities in four areas of print and broadcast journalism: writing, graphics, management, and ethics. The faculty teaches beginning and midcareer professionals as well as news executives, publishes teaching tools such as this book, and conducts educational and research projects, all of which seek the same goal: to raise levels of excellence in newspapers and the communications media generally.

Robert J. Haiman, President
The Poynter Institute

Acknowledgments

The Baltimore Sun, Richard O'Mara, and
  Roger Simon
Chicago Tribune and Kenneth Knox
The Bolivar Commercial and Wayne Nicholas
The Courier-Journal and Michael Jennings
The Miami Herald and Martin Merzer
The Muskegon Chronicle and Clayton
  Hardiman
The New York Times and Charles Klaveness
Philadelphia Daily News and Richard Aregood
The Philadelphia Inquirer and Diane Pucin
The Providence Journal and Randall Richard
The Sacramento Bee and Sam Stanton
The Wall Street Journal, Jules Ned Crabb, and
  Dorothy Rabinowitz
The Washington Post and Gene Weingarten

Cover illustration by Ken Weightman

Contents

Leading readers to and through our stories

BY DON FRY

Copy editors are the most important writers in the newsroom because they create paths to lead readers to the story. Without a good headline, cutline, and layout, readers never reach the golden prose in the lead.

This year, the ASNE Distinguished Writing Awards recognizes copy editors for the first time, with its new Headline Writing category. And just as copy editors pull readers down *to* the story, the winners in the other four categories lead readers *through* their stories.

HEADS FIT TO PRINT

Charles Klaveness of *The New York Times* is the first copy editor to win the ASNE Distinguished Writing Award. He draws readers to the lead with a combination of brightly worded headlines, cutlines, and pullouts.

Klaveness wrote this prize headline:

Where the V.S.O.P. Goes Down A.S.A.P.

to entice readers to this lead:

HONG KONG, Oct. 27—In this British colony of six million people, most of them Chinese, the preferred drink is fine aged French Cognac, not served neat in classic snifters but in tall tumblers, often over ice or mixed with fruit juice or soft drinks. But wine merchants and restaurateurs never criticize Hong Kong's unconventional approach to Cognac because, after all, they are dealing with the greatest Cognac drinkers in the world.

That headline lifts only one word from the lead: "the." Writers resent copy editors stealing the best words of their leads, and readers dislike reading essentially the same words twice. But Klaveness's headline focuses the whole story, not just the top, and captures the meaning and playful tone.

This headline presupposes reader familiarity with "V.S.O.P.," probably a safe bet in the feature section of the *The New York Times*. Klaveness plays with rhythm, rhyme, and even the visual shape of the acronyms as he adds "A.S.A.P.," which comes obliquely from a quotation three-quarters through the story: "We drink it very quickly from very large glasses." That same quotation also generated the pullout: "The two-fisted Cognac drinkers of Hong Kong," although the word "two-fisted" never appears in the story.

O BRAVE OLD WORLD

Dorothy Rabinowitz of *The Wall Street Journal* won the prize in Commentary for five columns and previews of television shows. She believes that American culture has gone badly awry, and she leads her readers on horrific little ventures through modern life.

One column, entitled "Welcome to Gotham," gives advice to Democrats about to attend their national nominating convention in a New York City gone mad:

NEW YORK—To the Democrats: a hearty New York greeting. Be assured, you are in for some fun in the city known to the world as the Big Apple or—its more recent name—Calcutta by the Hudson.

Rabinowitz conducts a tour of city hazards, such as bicyclists speeding on sidewalks, deafening boomboxes, cabbies (surly and probably armed), subway beggars, mental patients on buses, and, the final assault on her sensibilities:

Here in this neighborhood of expensive co-ops and townhouses, panhandlers stand five to a block. They are white, black and Hispanic or, as the mayor might say, part of the gorgeous mosaic. They are also pros.

She finds the presidential campaign especially excruciating (later, the right man lost) and blasts talk-show campaigning, especially "reverent formalities from television interviewers talking to presidential aspirants." Larry King and David Frost fail to kill off the barbarians, Perot and Clinton.

Wrapping herself in irony and angst, she laments the whole democratic process:

> No, there is hardly any doubt: The television talk shows have done their job presenting the candidates these many months. The question is whether we can ever forgive them for doing so, and whether we can, knowing all we know, drag ourselves to the polls.

SIMPLY OUTRAGEOUS

Richard Aregood of the *Philadelphia Daily News* has set a record by winning the award for Editorial Writing for the third time. Aregood has a well-deserved reputation as the most direct editorialist in the world, who always says what he means.

His editorials open with strong leads and end with strong kickers, and he draws his readers from beginning to end with uncompromising language. Here's the lead on a piece about George Bush's pardon for Caspar Weinberger:

> Great. Now we've got the criminals forgiving themselves. Even Richard Nixon, the Prince of Darkness himself, had the good taste to find some poor boob to blow out the charges against him.
>
> Too chancy for a sleaze like George Bush. Or maybe he knew that Bill Clinton wasn't likely to indulge himself in self-destructive stupidity like honest but dim Gerry Ford was.

When's the last time your paper printed phrases like "the Prince of Darkness himself," "some poor boob," "a sleaze like George

Bush," or "self-destructive stupidity"? Any reader reading such phrases at the top expects more to come, and keeps reading, and comes to language like this: "The fact is the policy was a criminal policy, administered in secret by criminals." And: "You cannot be a patriot while believing this great nation should ignore its own greatness and its own laws and behave like some homicidal junta."

And the reader arrives, hammered by all this straight talk and clear vision, at a typical Aregood kicker: "Now Bush has reached bottom. He pardoned himself."

TO THE DEATH

Sam Stanton of *The Sacramento Bee* won the prize for Deadline Writing with a story of the first execution in California in 25 years. Stanton leads readers through an eyewitness account, but hides his own role as that eyewitness. He follows George Orwell's injunction that "good prose is like a window pane," by never describing his own reactions and avoiding the first person.

Stanton frames the condemned man's last night with three opening paragraphs:

SAN QUENTIN—In the end, Robert Alton Harris seemed determined to go peacefully, a trait that had eluded him in the 39 violent and abusive years he spent on Earth.

As the cyanide fumes rose up to his face in the San Quentin gas chamber, he inhaled deeply and stared straight ahead, barely moving until death throes convulsed his body.

His trademark smirk was gone, replaced by a haunting look of sadness spawned by one last hellish night of fighting for his life and two predawn journeys to the gas chamber.

That passage has an invisible observer reacting inside it, in the verb "seemed," and in the phrases "a *haunting* look of sadness" and "one last *hellish* night" [my italics].

Stanton guides his readers with framing sentences like this: "But the events preceding his death were on a fine line between delayed justice and mental torture." And then he uses straight chronological telling, ticked along with constant time markers: "Scheduled to die at 12:01 a.m. Tuesday, Harris had begun Monday resigned to his fate...."

At the very end, with Harris officially dead, "the witnesses filed outside, into the bright sunlight." Not "*I* filed outside with the witnesses," or "*We* witnesses filed outside...." Stanton stays out of his readers' way and lets them witness the death.

TRACKING THE PHANTOM

Mike Jennings of the Louisville *Courier-Journal* won the prize in Non-Deadline Writing for a five-part series on his search for the father who abandoned him and his mother shortly after World War II. Jennings uses the suspense of his search to lead readers through each story, enhanced by images of a ghost that haunts him, and desolate landscapes. Like a good detective character in a thriller, he keeps sharing his puzzlement in the form of unanswered questions: Was the man in military records really his father? Did his father redeem his checkered military record? Was the father still alive? And finally:

What was I looking for? Did I simply want to see for once the face that, in my childhood, had seemed hidden behind the long, unwinding song of the cicada in the oak outside my bedroom window?

Was I hoping to find that a man as close to me as blood could make him had ascended, since he vanished from my mother's life, from the worst that was in him toward the best?

Or did I, as I'd told him, simply want the truth—believing the truth, whatever its contours, could set me free?

Jennings also leads his readers from one part of the series to the next with a series of cliff-hangers. At the end of the first two parts, he invokes his father's phantom, as in this kicker to part two:

> ...cutting short my search would not make my father's ghost go away. It would be right there in my footsteps, treading closer behind me than ever, until I turned and looked it in the face.

At the end of the third part, Jennings ends his first phone conversation with his father with an agreement to meet in person in the next installment. Now the problem: He meets his father in part four, so how can he entice the reader into reading one more story after this climax? Easy, he simply has the father retell his life and breaks in the middle of that narrative. Then the final section begins without a lead, throwing the readers directly into a tense scene of near disaster.

* * *

So copy editors and reporters use the same technique: They arrange the words to create paths our readers want to follow. And these five winners show paths of skill and power and dedication for all newswriters to follow.

BEST NEWSPAPER WRITING
1993

Michael Jennings
Non-Deadline Writing

MICHAEL JENNINGS, 46, an education reporter for *The Courier-Journal* in Louisville, Kentucky, won the ASNE Distinguished Writing Award for a five-part series on his search for his lost father.

Jennings was born in Winston-Salem, North Carolina. He is married to Leslie Scanlon, also a reporter at *The Courier-Journal*. He received a B.A. in psychology from the University of North Carolina at Chapel Hill in 1969, and an M.A. in English from the University of Virginia at Charlottesville in 1978. He joined *The Courier-Journal* in 1989.

Mike Jennings reconstructs the complex trail that led him to his natural father, paths full of typically Southern intricate genealogies. We watch Mike's own emotional development as his mystery story unfolds.

Congratulations, Mike, for your skills as a writer and as a detective.

The search for my father: First of five parts

DECEMBER 27, 1992

After his mother's death, reporter Michael Jennings set out on a personal quest into the past. In a series of stories starting today, he describes the faint, winding trail that led him at last to a little windblown town on the Texas prairie.

In mid-August 1945, a few days after atomic bombs fell on Hiroshima and Nagasaki, a 29-year-old Marine climbed down from a train at a siding in eastern North Carolina.

He was bound for Camp Lejeune, where he would muster into a redistribution company. There, troops returning from duty assignments would be sorted and reassigned.

With the war's end in sight, many of the 31,000 Marines at the training base on the New River could look forward to a swift return to civilian life. But the lanky Marine—who, despite his years, wore only a private's stripes—knew he wasn't one of them.

For him, it had never truly begun. Having missed the fire and terror of the war itself, he could expect to share whatever hardship there was to be borne in its aftermath. At a time when ports were flooded with returning troops, he knew he'd probably be sent overseas.

Lean and high-waisted, with spidery legs, gaunt cheeks and hooded brown eyes, he fit the image of the seasoned leatherneck. But there were good reasons for his lowly rank. There was ample warrant for the Marines' asking more of him than they would of those who fought at Guadalcanal and Iwo Jima.

He knew the reasons, and he did not care to talk about them. But as he entered the swirl of war's-end activity at Lejeune, he did not know something equally important.

He did not know that an unmarried school-teacher, daughter of a school superintendent, was about to travel from a farm in the Carolina Piedmont to Wilmington, where she would take over a first-grade class of 42 children.

He did not know that he would meet her and that their encounter would make of him a ghost. The man himself remained very much alive. But his ghost haunted me for 46 years, until I saw it dissolve above fields of sprouting winter wheat on the plains of north Texas.

This is a ghost story.

It is also a detective yarn. And it is a cautionary tale, showing what forbidding shapes ghosts can assume before they reveal that they are nothing but the interplay of shadow, fear and dream.

My mother told me my name was Michael Johnson. Dimly, I understood that the name came to me from someone I either had not seen or could not remember. When I was 4, my mother married a man who taught at her school.

Presently she told me to call myself by his name, Jennings. When my brother was born, I was told I was just as much my father's son as he. I believed this so well that I was puzzled, years later, when my parents opened an official-looking envelope and announced that I was now legally Michael Jennings, son of Woodrow Jennings.

I hadn't been aware there was any doubt. Except that sometimes, when the rain on the tin roof of our farmhouse lengthened the interval between waking and sleep, something would whisper to me: "This man is all you will get as a father, and you should be grateful for him. He is kind and loving, in his pained, awkward way, and he will never leave us.

"But he is not your father. Your father is—somewhere else."

The summer I turned 13, my mother told me nearly all she would ever tell me about the man who gave me a name I had by then nearly forgotten.

He was in the Marines, he was from Texas, and he had been a truck driver. She told me he had Indian blood.

After he went away, she said, she heard from his mother that he was already married.

I think I remember her using the word big-amist. She said that, when she learned of her predicament, she thought of abortion, and of suicide.

She told me he had grown up being catered to by his mother and sisters. He was used to having his way.

Finally, she said with a bitterness I never saw in her again: "Don't you ever do to a girl what Bob Johnson did to me."

She never said anything like that to me again. There was never any sign she blamed me for the pain he caused her. But I couldn't forget that he had done something terrible to her, and that I was his son.

After that midsummer's day, his ghost never truly left me. For years, I might barely think of him consciously. And then some ignoble choice I had made would force me to stop and turn, and I would see a faint presence treading in my shadow. And I would wonder how, unsensed, it had been altering the course of my life all along.

From somewhere in my childhood, I have dredged up this dream. I am playing in the yard, and I hear the roar of a huge engine struggling up our hill from the creek bottom. It is a giant tractor-trailer rig, something that would be seen on our rural road only if the driver were lost or pursuing some unlikely mission.

With a squeal of the air brakes, the truck halts between the yard and the log barn that my great-grandfather built. The driver, a lean-faced man with high cheekbones, turns and gazes at me somberly. The truck rocks back-ward and forward, rolling downhill a few feet, then lurching ahead with a spurt of black smoke from the stack above the cab.

Finally, the driver grasps the wheel with the hunch-shouldered, hand-and-forearm grip that truck drivers use, and the rig rumbles onward over the brow of our hill, past my aunt's house, seeming to shake the earth with the hammering of its engine.

In the summer of 1987, I watched my mother die.

From Friday night until Monday morning, as she drifted in and out of consciousness and relatives and friends came to see her for the last time, my sister-in-law and I held her upright in a recliner chair on what had once been the porch and was now an enclosed room. The chair was in nearly the same spot where Mother had told me, all those years before, never to do what my father had done.

When we got her to the hospital on Monday and they pierced her hand and started the anesthesia, her eyes remained fixed on me as she began her slow drift away from us.

For years, as she turned more and more to television evangelists and I pursued interests that were wholly secular, the channel of love between us had grown constricted. There were times when we both struggled to find the word that would let it flow free and strong again, but neither of us could quite remember it.

As I gazed into her eyes over the two days until she died, the constriction dissolved, and no word was necessary. Her eyes looked incredibly youthful and tender.

A year and a half after she died, I decided I would track my ghost to its lair. I would find what substance lay behind its phantom shape.

The man I had good cause to call my true father had died in 1980. Finding Robert Johnson, I thought, could harm no one still living.

There were two people still alive whom I was neglecting to count. I was one of them.

I had not yet met the other. At least not in the flesh.

TOMORROW: The writer describes his search for clues to his father's identity—and the shock of what he finally found.

Observations and questions

1) This story has an eight-paragraph lead ("In mid-August...north Texas."). List the expectations such a lead arouses in the reader for this story and for the series. Discuss the advantages and disadvantages for the reader of setting such expectations.

2) Jennings begins his ghost theme in the eighth paragraph ("He did not know...north Texas.") in an almost mystical passage about what his father could not know. Track this ghost theme through all five parts of the series, and study how Jennings uses it.

3) The author develops his ghost image in paragraphs nine and ten:

> This is a ghost story.
>
> It is also a detective yarn. And it is a cautionary tale, showing what forbidding shapes ghosts can assume before they reveal that they are nothing but the interplay of shadow, fear and dream.

Move this passage to the top and think about how it would function as a lead for the story and for the series.

4) At what point does the reader learn what this story and series are about? How could you tell the reader earlier to prevent impatience?

5) In the middle of this story, Jennings captures his childhood confusion about the identity of his real father in several confusing paragraphs ("My mother told ...somewhere else."). How can we express confusion without confusing our readers?

6) Jennings told me that the dream in this piece ("From somewhere...its engine.") is nearly fiction. Since we rarely print fiction in newspapers, even in a piece this literary, should we frame this section to tell the reader not to take it straight? How?

7) Jennings needs a compelling ending to his first story so readers will want to read the next segment. Study this ending and think of other ways to hold the readers.

The search for my father: Second of five parts

DECEMBER 28, 1992

Yesterday, reporter Michael Jennings related the little he learned in childhood about his father. He told how that knowledge haunted him and how he decided, after his mother's death, that he would track his father down.

The search for the ghost who was my father reminded me that there are no clearly marked, well-lighted pathways into the past.

Like a descent into a cave, my progress yielded shadowy half-glimpses and led over sudden, blind precipices. What I found in the way of crystalline fact posed the question *Why?*, but left it to echo unanswered.

I thought I already knew the worst. I thought my father deceived and abandoned my mother. I thought he married her when he was already married to someone else. I thought I inherited his name.

None of that turned out to be quite true.

In the winter of 1989, I got a copy of my hospital birth record and looked up my birth announcement in my hometown newspaper. Both identified me as Michael Johnson, son of J. R. Johnson, but the hospital file recorded my mother by her maiden name.

The newspaper announcement told me something I hadn't known: When I was born in July 1946, my father was with the Marines in China.

I asked for the record of my adoption by my stepfather, and got the same rude rebuff that adoptees typically get in states where they are denied the facts of their existence.

I hired a genealogist and a lawyer. From the North Carolina archives, I got a list of the teachers at the Wilmington school where my mother taught first grade in 1945-46.

Piecing together information from those sources, I concluded that neither I nor my mother ever legally bore my father's name. I gave up trying to locate a marriage license.

Without either that or adoption records, my only hope for tracing my father lay in military files.

All I knew was that he was a Marine, he was in China when I was born and he must have been in North Carolina the previous fall.

An officer at Camp Lejeune suggested I try the Marine Corps Historical Center in Washington, D.C., the archive for muster rolls—the monthly rosters of all Marines on duty.

An archivist at the historical center told me there were thousands of Marines in North China after World War II. Locating one with so common a name as J. Robert Johnson, he said, could take months, unless I knew his unit.

I visited the historical center in October 1990 and picked up a pamphlet on the Marines' operations in North China from 1945 to 1949. From it I learned that in June 1946, the month before my birth, the Marines in China reorganized into three units with an authorized strength of 24,252 men.

I pondered the odds against finding my father by other means. I'd stood next to the file cabinets containing the muster rolls, and I knew that the key to the secret of his identity was in there somewhere. I felt the task was manageable: I had to scan the July 1946 muster rolls for fewer than 25,000 Marines.

I arranged to go back to Washington in November and spend a week.

The Marine Corps Historical Center faces the parade ground of the Washington Navy Yard, a cluster of severe white brick buildings by the Anacostia River.

It took me 44 years to get there. It will take me at least that long to get over it.

Within four hours, I found my father.

I came across two Robert Johnsons and two John Johnsons before hitting on Pvt. James R.

Johnson, service number 297916. He was a light antiaircraft gun crewman in Company B, 1st Battalion, 1st Marines, 1st Marine Division, stationed in Tientsin, China. A footnote said that on July 24, the day after my birth, Pvt. Johnson left Tientsin for discharge in the United States.

The Marines are meticulous record-keepers. The muster rolls show when each man entered a unit, where he came from and where he went when he left.

Going back month by month, I found that James R. Johnson joined the 1st Marines in January from the 94th Replacement Draft. I jumped to the muster rolls for Camp Lejeune and found him there, in a headquarters company, in September 1945.

For most of a day I struggled to keep him in focus amid the kaleidoscopic flux of a big military base at war's end. I found him under four unit headings in September alone.

As I traced him from unit to unit without being able to break free of September, I sensed I was straining against a barrier thrown up by something that did not wish to be known.

Finally I broke through, and stopped dead in the sudden chill.

Pvt. Johnson's assignment to a redistribution battalion reached back into August. A footnote to the monthly muster roll said that, on Aug. 14, he had joined the unit from the Naval Prison in Portsmouth, N.H.

From that point on, it became painfully easy to trace him backward in time—though time, for him, seemed frozen. Month by month, he was there in the prison's muster rolls, always with a notation that meant "confined, serving sentence."

When the Marine archive closed for the day, I walked numbly out the gate of the Navy Yard and down Ninth Street to a bar. I quickly drank one beer and ordered another.

For the two years since I'd begun trying to add flesh to my ghost, I'd nursed the hope of finding some counterbalance to what I already knew about him. Perhaps the notation, "awarded Silver Star Medal for conspicuous gallantry...." Some sign that, like Lucifer, had he not shown so brightly, he could never have fallen so low.

Now that hope was gone. I didn't yet know what landed him in prison, but it was clear that his crime against my mother was of a piece with the rest of him.

During the rest of that week, I traced him backward and forward in the muster rolls until I had a finished picture of an utterly sorry military career.

He enlisted in Los Angeles in September 1940. In January 1941, while assigned to a headquarters company in San Diego, he was away without leave for four days. His commander sentenced him to 20 days' solitary confinement on bread and water, with full rations every third day.

He was classed as a "prisoner at large" until a cell became available. Apparently he was loosely guarded; on Feb. 12 he went "over the hill" again.

This time he stayed gone for two years, two months and 28 days.

He turned up in Los Angeles in May 1943 and was held for trial by general court-martial.

In the summer of 1943, James R. Johnson's old unit, the Headquarters and Service Company of the 8th Marines, 2nd Marine Division, was deployed at Paekakariki on New Zealand's northern island. Its men were out of range of the nearest combat, but not as far from it as Pvt. Johnson would be.

He was tried June 8, convicted of desertion and sentenced to six years in prison and a dishonorable discharge. The sentence exceeded the permissible maximum and about four months were shaved off.

He was imprisoned from October 1943 until August 1945, first at Mare Island off San Francisco, then at Portsmouth. The day after the

atomic bomb fell on Hiroshima he was returned to duty on 12 months' probation.

At Camp Lejeune, he trained as a projector
operator-repairman, then as a light antiaircraft
gunner. On Dec. 7, 1945, four years after the
Japanese attacked Pearl Harbor, he and about
1,745 other Marines departed Norfolk, Va., on
board the USS *Wakefield*.

They were bound for a still-smoldering the-
ater of the recently ended war—North China,
where the Marines helped repatriate more than
a half-million Japanese. While striving to
avoid combat, the Marines also tried to bolster
the Nationalist regime against the onslaught of
communist forces under Mao Tse-tung.

While James R. Johnson was in China, the
Marines steadily scaled back their operations
there, as men fresh from boot camp replaced
combat veterans. By May, their mission had
dwindled to little more than guard duty.

On July 25, 1946, Pvt. Johnson sailed from
Taku on the USS *General H. W. Butner*. On
August 9, he was back in San Diego, where his
disastrous Marine Corps career had begun six
years earlier.

On October 22, he returned to civilian life
with an honorable discharge—a sign that, during his probation at least, he'd finally proven
himself a passable Marine.

I had more time than I needed for my research.
I spent part of it wandering through the museum
on the center's first floor, gazing into glass cases
at artifacts of combat in the jungles of Central
America, on Pacific atolls, in Vietnam.

There was no glass case with reminders of
the way Pvt. J. R. Johnson spent his war.

It occurred to me that I could quietly close
the book on Robert Johnson. I knew enough,
I thought. Perhaps too much.

There were two problems with that idea. One
was that I wasn't dead sure the James R.
Johnson in the muster rolls was who I thought
he was. The other was that cutting short my
search would not make my father's ghost go

away. It would be right there in my footsteps, treading closer behind me than ever, until I turned and looked it in the face.

TOMORROW: The writer follows the last turnings of the trail, and one August evening, hears the voice of a ghost.

Observations and questions

1) Every lead in any part of a series introduces its own story and the remaining stories in the series. Study how Jennings opens part two, and think about other ways to pull readers into reading this part and all the parts.

2) How can we assist readers who may not have read part one?

3) Which threads of meaning and imagery has Jennings carried over from part one? Why?

4) The search for his father actually begins in this section. Jennings tells his detective story by following the steps that led to the final discovery. What other ways can you think of for organizing this complex series? Think about their advantages and disadvantages.

5) In the middle of this piece, Jennings gives us a paragraph of data:

> I came across two Robert Johnsons and two John Johnsons before hitting on Pvt. James R. Johnson, service number 297916. He was a light antiaircraft gun crewman in Company B, 1st Battalion, 1st Marines, 1st Marine Division, stationed in Tientsin, China. A footnote said that on July 24, the day after my birth, Pvt. Johnson left Tientsin for discharge in the United States.

Why does Jennings tell us all this minutiae, even his father's service number? How does he provide all this detail without turning readers off?

6) The author introduces a new theme, his hopes to find a worthy father, perhaps a war hero, just as he discovers his father's imprisonment and "utterly sorry military career." Consider the different effects if he separated these two subjects.

7) This piece ends with an emotional and literary cliffhanger. How else could Jennings end it to keep his readers moving forward to the next installment?

The search for my father: Third of five parts

DECEMBER 29, 1992

In earlier articles, reporter Michael Jennings told how he began the search for his father, and how the discovery of an ugly secret—his father's desertion from the Marines—tempted him to abandon it.

Pvt. James R. Johnson, Marine Corps deserter and almost certainly my father, eluded me for nearly two more years after my heart-sickening journey through the microfilmed muster rolls in November 1990.

I sent his serial number and dates of service to the National Personnel Records Center in St. Louis, the warehouse for the files of America's 20th-century military veterans.

The response form confirmed his middle name was Robert. It also told me that he was born May 1, 1916, that he'd finished one year of high school and that he had two dependents —a wife, Emily, and a son, James Robert Jr.

It showed that he earned a few run-of-the-mill medals. A section headed "If veteran is deceased" was crossed out, suggesting he might be alive.

The Veterans Affairs Department had no record of him. Apparently he never sought benefits.

I thought my mother had said he was from Texas, but the records showed he enlisted in Los Angeles and made his home there after discharge. I decided to concentrate my search on California and queried the vital-statistics office in Sacramento for birth, marriage and death records.

Nothing turned up, except the unexpected: As my fiancee and I thumbed through my mother's photograph albums, searching for pictures to use in a wedding video, we found a photo of a hollow-eyed man in uniform standing in front of a cracked brick wall. On the back, Mother had written "Daddy" and "Made in China" and "Summer of 1946."

I knew the National Personnel Records Center could provide more information if I could pry loose its privacy restrictions. Last June, I spoke to R. M. Schrader, chief of its Navy Reference Branch, which handles Marine records.

I told him I thought I could make a convincing case that I was the natural son of a man I'd found in the muster rolls. I asked if he could release more information on that basis. He said he'd see what he could do.

I sent him a letter, my birth announcement, muster rolls and other documents. Two weeks later, I got from Schrader enough information to propel me to the end of my search.

It included a copy of the record booklet that accompanied Pvt. James R. Johnson throughout his enlistment.

The first page bore Robert Johnson's enlistment photograph. That just about killed off any doubt. It could have been my own photo at the same age.

Page two showed he was born at Whitt, Texas, listed his home of record as Newcastle, Texas, and named his mother, of Wichita Falls, Texas, as his next of kin. So I'd been wrong not to trust my recollection that he was a Texan.

A record of the court-martial showed Pvt. Johnson had pleaded innocent to the desertion charge. An attached note said the Argonne Van & Storage Co. in Los Angeles reported that— while working for the company the month before he was turned in as a deserter—he abandoned a moving van in San Diego and absconded with $112. The note said he claimed he took the money in lieu of overdue wages.

So he was, arguably, a thief as well as a deserter.

I wrote to the Texas Bureau of Vital Statistics, asking for the birth certificate of a James Robert Johnson who was born in Whitt to Ruby Johnson on May 1, 1916.

What came in response was an extraordinary document. Titled "delayed certificate of birth," it was issued in 1977, and it showed that James Robert Johnson was then living in Albuquerque, N. M.

Most important was the list of documents he'd presented to prove he was born when and where he said he was: his Social Security application, his military record, a certificate of employment from Consolidated Freightways and an affidavit from his father.

I called the Albuquerque office of Consolidated Freightways, a nationwide trucking company, and was referred to Mark Mallory, manager of the relay station at Tucumcari, N. M.

"I'm familiar with a J. R. Johnson" who would be about the age of the man I was hunting, Mallory said. He said Bob Johnson, as he called him, had retired in the late 1970s after "a fairly long history with this company" in Albuquerque and Los Angeles.

It was from Mallory that I heard the first kind words I'd ever heard about my father:

"Bob was a good worker. He was an honest person, loyal, and had a good company attitude."

After retiring, Bob Johnson had bought a truck and moved to the Texas Panhandle town of Dalhart, Mallory said.

The next day, after checking with two other men who knew Bob Johnson, Mallory told me he'd remarried. His previous wife had died in Albuquerque, Mallory said.

When last heard from, about three years ago, Bob Johnson was driving a gravel truck near Vega, Texas, he said.

I told Mallory that I'd mail him a photograph and call him again to find if it looked like the man he knew.

I got the numbers of two gravel companies in Vega. On August 11, a Tuesday, I sprinted through the last few turns in the trail.

A woman at Vega Sand & Gravel said J. R. Johnson had worked there nine years ago but now hauled grain for two sisters in Canyon, Texas.

"We call him 'Buckshot,'" the woman said. "That's his CB handle."

His wife's name was Marie, she said. She had his Social Security number, and it matched the one I'd found on his birth certificate.

She gave me Bob Johnson's home phone number in Hereford, Texas. She said he might not be home before 8 p.m.

I called Mallory again. He'd gotten the copy I'd sent him of the first page of the Marine Corps record, which bore an enlistment photo and signature.

The photo, he said, "could quite easily be Bob Johnson.... And the signature on that is about as recognizable as the picture."

When I got home that evening, a message from Marie Johnson was on my telephone recorder. The woman at Vega Sand & Gravel had told her I was looking for her husband.

I waited until 8 o'clock, Texas time. If he was alive, I wanted above all else to see him. I didn't want to say anything that would jeopardize that.

Marie answered the phone. I said I thought her husband and I might be related. I said I planned to come to Texas and wanted to see him.

"Well, he's here," she said. "Would you like to speak to him?"

His voice wasn't quite a ghost-voice. It sounded weathered, but not faint; wary, but not alarmed.

I told him my name. "Well, what sort of relation does it involve here?" he said. "I don't recall any relations by that name."

I said I wasn't sure. I could tell him my travel plans later, I said.

"Have you lived in that (part of the) country all your life?" he said.

I dodged that question too. I said I'd call again.

"Where are you originally from, Michael?"

"I'm originally from North Carolina."

Very quietly he said: "I see." He cleared his
throat. "Now I think I know what the relationship is."

I told him that I meant him no harm, that I
only wanted to know the truth. I told him my
mother was dead.

He said he could see why it would be good
for us to meet.

"In my case, you probably haven't got an
awful lot of time," he said. "So if we're going
to do it, we'd better get it done."

*TOMORROW: In a dim parking lot at the
end of a little prairie town, the writer meets a
ghost.*

Observations and questions

1) Part three has no lead; it just starts telling the story. Compose several leads for this part, and then compare them for effect with Jennings's opening.

2) This story and the whole series have parallel chronological structures: Jennings's own life, his father's life, and his search to find his father. Since we know quite early that Jennings *did* find his father, how does he maintain suspense? How does he keep the three chronological tracks from becoming confusing or boring?

3) Jennings describes his father's picture from his service record in the 12th paragraph: "The first page bore Robert Johnson's enlistment photograph. That just about killed off any doubt. It could have been my own photo at the same age." Discuss this passage in terms of the theme of Jennings's search for his own identity.

4) Much of this detective work involves drudgery and small detail. Study how Jennings uses little touches to make even the smallest discoveries dramatic.

5) This piece has 12 people in it, just a small part of the cast of characters in the whole series. Analyze how Jennings spreads characters out, demotes some to just names ("Ruby Johnson") or just identifications ("two sisters"), and develops others fully. Particularly notice how he reintroduces people readers have met before, but may have forgotten.

6) Jennings recorded the telephone conversation at the end of this story, which he says is shortened but nearly verbatim. Notice the interplay of paraphrase and direct quoting, and the light attribution. What makes this scene seem real to the readers?

7) Journalists tend to describe inner states from outward signs, like this:
>   Very quietly he said: "I see." He cleared his throat.
>   "Now I think I know what the relationship is."
Imagine this passage in novelistic style, with the author looking into the father's mind. Which works better and why?

The search for my father: Fourth of five parts

DECEMBER 30, 1992

In earlier articles, reporter Michael Jennings told how he was haunted by the little he knew of his father, and how his search for the truth led him to a town in the Texas panhandle.

As I boarded the plane to Texas, I glanced into the cockpit, where the pilot and co-pilot sat thigh-to-elbow, like jockeys, amid their myriad switches and warning lights.

I thought of all the James Robert Johnsons scattered across the continent, and of the difficulty, among all those winking or dimly pulsating lives, of reaching for the right one.

I thought of how a slight tilt of destiny's wheel might have allotted me some Bob Johnson other than the one who shirked his war, deceived a schoolteacher, went to China and had his hollow-eyed photograph taken there, and 46 years later spoke to me in a voice that sounded as dust-scoured as the arid Texas plains where I ran him to earth.

What was I looking for? Did I simply want to see for once the face that, in my childhood, had seemed hidden behind the long, unwinding song of the cicada in the oak outside my bedroom window?

Was I hoping to find that a man as close to me as blood could make him had ascended, since he vanished from my mother's life, from the worst that was in him toward the best?

Or did I, as I'd told him, simply want the truth—believing the truth, whatever its contours, could set me free?

The aircraft descended toward lionskin-colored plains beneath a leaden October sky pricked by the faint filigree spires of distant oil rigs. I rented a car in Amarillo, drove south to Canyon, then headed west through country where the brown of brittle silage crops was interspersed with the lush green of sprouting winter wheat.

A dust cloud blanketed the sunset at Hereford's eastern edge, where thousands of milling cattle were being fattened at the Southwest Feed Yard. I assumed the stench was also cattle; later, I learned it came from a sugar-beet processing plant.

I checked into my motel and called Marie Johnson. She said Bob wasn't home yet. She came in a red Plymouth Sundance and led me to a ranch-style house with a carport. Two dusty-looking trees had shed tiny leaves in the yard.

She sat on the couch. She said her granddaughter, whom she and Bob were raising, was away playing French horn with Hereford's high school marching band. The band was vying for its 32nd straight district title.

Marie said she thought Bob was scared to meet me. "He's an odd man," she said. She tilted her topknot of disheveled gray hair. "Are you odd?"

At 8 o'clock he still wasn't home. We got in her car and she drove to a paved lot at what seemed the edge of town. Several trucks and unhitched trailers were parked there.

"Can you see if that's a white one?" she said.

The cab and trailer she was squinting at were solid white. Beneath the cab's dome light, I could see a figure in a cap bent over the wheel.

Yes, he's scared to meet you, she said.

We got out, and I followed her toward the cab. The man frowned down at her, but he didn't seem to see me. His wizened face seemed to peer out from between his hunched shoulders.

I stepped up on a latticed metal running board and looked in at the averted, weathered face with its high, tilted cheekbones, narrow mustache and outsized ears. His flattened nose had whorled edges, like those on a Mayan bust. Compared to his compact torso, his dungaree-clad shanks looked astonishingly long and spindle-thin. His belt was lined with little bronze medallions and fastened with a rectangular white buckle.

He was writing with slow, precise strokes in a log book. I reached my hand through the open window. He glanced up at me through gold-rimmed bifocals, showing no surprise, and lifted a hand to mine.

There, in a dim parking lot at the end of a little lost prairie town, I touched my father.

He flicked a hand toward the dashboard. For the first time I saw the sudden, impish smile that turns his eyes to slits.

"How do you like my truck?" he said. The woman he worked for, he said, bought it for him new last February. There were more than 80,000 miles on the odometer.

"And nobody's put a mile on her but me," he said.

Then another quicksilver change.

You know, he said, I came to North Carolina and saw you once. He held up his hands; his forearms looked as mottled and stringy as strips of jerky. "You were about this long."

I got back in Marie's car. "That broke the ice," she said. "He'll be all right now."

That night and the next day, a Sunday, Bob Johnson told me how his life had gone, and how it touched mine.

Listening to him as he sat at his dining table, smoking cigarettes and talking on in his raspy drawl, was like watching a dream edit reality. Only this was reality editing my own long dream.

He was born in Parker County, west of Fort Worth, the eldest of seven children, and the only boy.

When he was 9, his appendix ruptured. He turned blue under the fingernails, and he heard beautiful music and his family gathered around him. But the music went away and eventually he rode an interurban rail car home from the hospital in Mineral Wells.

His family blew like tumbleweed across the hardscrabble landscape.

"We were poor, like in *poor* poor," his oldest sister, Vida Mae, told me later. Sometimes, she said, the children would stay out of school to pick cotton, dragging a long "ducking" sack as they stooped or crawled down the rows.

In the Depression's pit, with his father out of work, Robert Johnson quit high school and started driving trucks. In 1940, he bought a car, drove west, worked for a while near Los Angeles and enlisted in the Marines 10 days after Franklin Roosevelt signed the draft law.

Fresh from boot camp in San Diego, he married a woman he'd known in Texas, then discovered she was living with another man.

"And I just blew up, went berserk," he said. Within a few days, he started a liaison with another woman. In January, he deserted from the Marines, moved in with his new companion and went back to driving trucks in Los Angeles.

Two years and three months later, he said, he walked up to a civilian policeman and turned himself in, feeling "it was something that had to be faced up to."

By then he'd fathered one son, but he hadn't married the boy's mother.

While imprisoned at Portsmouth, New Hampshire, he persuaded a psychiatrist to change a recommendation that he not be returned to duty. He was put in the naval prison's retraining battalion.

"I've always been, secretly maybe, a little proud that I did salvage something," he said.

But his private life remained a shambles.

Arriving at Camp Lejeune at the war's end, he knew he'd have to serve at least another year. With returning troops flooding the ports, he assumed he'd replace one of them overseas.

Sometime in early fall 1945, Robert Johnson and a friend met two schoolteachers in Wilmington. "And my friend started going with the other girl, and I...started an association with your mother."

In late October, he got a one-week furlough. He used it to hop a military flight to Las Vegas,

Nevada, where he married the mother of his first son.

He didn't tell my mother about that.

He also impregnated a female Marine. He said his commander put him on the replacement draft for China to get him out of that jam.

After he left, the woman miscarried.

He had my mother's car, a green Dodge that wouldn't go into reverse, on base when he learned he would ship out the next morning. He drove it to her in Wilmington, and she drove him partway back.

He didn't know she was pregnant. He found out months later, in China, when he got a long letter spelling out the arrangements she'd made.

"And the night I learned that, I got drunk and got hold of some ammunition and was attempting to blow my brains out in the barracks when somebody stopped me."

He was at Peking, in charge of a detail sent there to clean up an old rifle range, when the Marines started trying to ship him home for discharge. With his stateside affairs more chaotic than ever, he didn't want to go.

Twice he managed to be away on pass when troop ships left. The third time, military police grabbed him in Tientsin, whisked him to Peking to get his gear and had him aboard ship by nightfall.

Home, discharged, jobless, estranged from his wife, Robert Johnson decided he wanted to see the schoolteacher he'd left in Wilmington and the child whose existence, revealed to him half a world away, had sent him in search of a clip for his rifle.

Around the end of 1946, he drove a quirky Hudson cross-country. The cork inserts in the clutch burned out; he bought a sack of bottle corks at a drugstore in Tupelo, Mississippi, stuck them in the clutch and drove on.

He found his way to a rural crossroads near the farm where my mother lived with her parents. He rented a room.

It was dark, though not late night, when he came to our house. He was there "just a few minutes, actually," he told me. "You were in an upstairs room, as I recall."

He said I was asleep and never saw him.

He and my mother drove down the road and talked a while. "I think we more or less decided...it was better if I went on back and stayed out of things."

He went back to his rented room, drove west the next morning and never saw her again.

Later he learned that his mother and mine had corresponded. That was how Mother learned Robert Johnson already had a wife.

"And that has haunted me for all these years—knowing the trauma that she had to endure through all this," he said.

"I didn't want anything to taint any opportunity she had to salvage, you know, her life—the whole thing. And it wasn't easy.

"I went through that area many times during the years while she was still alive, and was sorely tempted to contact somebody. But this reason was uppermost in my mind...and I stayed away—stayed out of it."

TOMORROW: A ghost disappears. In its place, the writer sees only an old man struggling to do the best he can.

Observations and questions

1) Writers of suspense stories delay the reader to build anticipation. Think about the opening of this part in terms of setting a scene and holding the readers back.

2) Paragraphs four through six pose a series of questions:

What was I looking for? Did I simply want to see for once the face that, in my childhood, had seemed hidden behind the long, unwinding song of the cicada in the oak outside my bedroom window?

Was I hoping to find that a man as close to me as blood could make him had ascended, since he vanished from my mother's life, from the worst that was in him toward the best?

Or did I, as I'd told him, simply want the truth—believing the truth, whatever its contours, could set me free?

Readers expect answers to questions posed. Track the questions to the end of the series to see if and how Jennings answers them.

3) Jennings writes very literary landscapes throughout the series, for example:

The aircraft descended toward lionskin-colored plains beneath a leaden October sky pricked by the faint filigree spires of distant oil rigs. I rented a car in Amarillo, drove south to Canyon, then headed west through country where the brown of brittle silage crops was interspersed with the lush green of sprouting winter wheat.

What effects can you imagine these landscapes have on the readers? Do they enhance or detract from the search framework?

4) Jennings and his father come together figuratively in this paragraph:

Marie said she thought Bob was scared to meet me. "He's an odd man," she said. She tilted her topknot of disheveled gray hair. "Are you odd?"

Why doesn't Jennings answer that question, either to Marie or for the reader? Or does he?

5) As Jennings finally meets his father, the action stops for a long paragraph of description ("I stepped up

...white buckle."). Think about this paragraph in terms of delaying the reader, capturing an important moment in the author's saga, and snapping the ghost into focus.

6) See if you can revise the climactic sentence of this series: "There, in a dim parking lot at the end of a little lost, prairie town, I touched my father." First, make it sparer. Then more literary and ornate. Then delete it. What effects does each revision create? What do you gain and lose?

7) The second half of this segment begins a long chronology from the father's point of view. How does Jennings keep it interesting after all the earlier chronologies?

8) Now that we've met the ghost-father, how does Jennings entice us to read one more installment?

The search for my father: Last of five parts

DECEMBER 31, 1992

In earlier articles, reporter Michael Jennings described how he tracked down and finally met the father he had never seen.

About three years ago, Bob Johnson was making a late-night haul in sub-zero weather when he stopped in Hereford, intending to change trailers and head back to San Angelo. He was less than a mile from home, but nobody knew he was in town.

The trailer's release bar was stuck. When he lunged against it, it broke and he fell, shattering his hip and knocking himself unconscious.

I like to think that, as he lay there, my mother's ghost came to him from deep within the frozen earth.

"Bob," she whispered to him. "You've got to wake up, or you'll die here.

"I forgive you, if that's what's bothering you. You gave me a life that meant more to me than my own. Let me give you back yours."

When he came to, he looked down and saw his left foot was turned at an impossible angle. He tried to stand, but pain bludgeoned him down.

He was lying to the right of the cab, and he knew the door on that side was locked. He dragged himself with his hands around to the driver's side. Somehow he lifted himself inside.

He couldn't raise anyone on his VHF radio, but on the citizens band he reached a traveler who stopped and made the emergency call.

The paramedics, fearing the bone would pierce an artery, took a long time removing him from the cab. A surgeon in Amarillo did a complete hip replacement.

Now, at 76, he winces when he lies on his back to grease his trailer's axles. "This getting up and down's an ordeal for me," he said.

It's an ordeal he undergoes every week. And every morning in the fall, when the grain has to be moved from silos to feed lots, he gets up at 4 a.m. and heads out of town by 6. He drives at least 500 miles a day, eats lunch in his cab and gets home, too tired to shower, between 8 and 10 p.m.

Six days a week he does that. On the seventh, he pulls on his coveralls, grabs his grease gun and hitches himself painfully beneath his trailer.

Even Marie, his 67-year-old wife, "doesn't know any of this dark history," he said after telling me of his desertion from the Marines and his term in naval prisons. "I've learned even to deny it to myself."

His life's been a failure, he said.

But when I add it up, I get no such simple sum.

There's been plenty of failure, certainly. And it didn't stop the day he drove away from our farmhouse, heading back to California after coming cross-country to see my mother for the last time, and me for what he thought would be the only time.

The car he'd driven to North Carolina was repossessed. He went back to driving a truck and "being a loner, drifting from place to place."

His wife, who had borne him three sons, charged him with desertion. He dodged the charge for a time, but eventually it stuck. He served a year's sentence at a road camp near Los Angeles.

When his eldest son graduated from high school, he bought the boy a suit and a graduation gift. He'd heard nothing more from any of his four sons until I tracked him down.

In 1958, soon after his release from the road camp, he met Leona Clement, the West Coast sales manager for a New York furrier. They married the same year, and he went to work for Consolidated Freightways.

The marriage and the job lasted 20 years, until Leona died of emphysema. During that time, he got a private pilot's license, bought and flew airplanes and helled around on a motorcycle with a black poodle that was addicted to high-speed travel. The dog flew, too, and would happily stick its head out the plane's window, its ears streaming in the 130-mph rush of air.

He served two terms as union shop steward, and Consolidated gave him a belt full of safe-driving medallions for almost two million accident-free miles.

Twice he chartered a hospital plane to fly Leona from Albuquerque to California for treatment. When she died, he filed for bankruptcy, retired and made a down payment on a truck, which he later lost.

Helping Leona fight her illness to the end, he said, was "one of my few major accomplishments." He said Leona told him that, after she died, he should marry Marie. He married her so soon after Leona's death, he said, that some thought it "almost indecent."

Since retiring, he's held a succession of trucking jobs in the Texas Panhandle around Dalhart, Vega and Hereford. He's lost three jobs and been denied one when insurers refused to cover him because of his age.

The young woman who employs him now, Rita Ward, pays extra to insure him. It's worth it because "he's a heck of a worker," she told me. "I mean, he'll go anywhere, do anything."

With what she pays him, his Teamsters pension and his and Marie's Social Security payments, "we're managing to squeak by fairly well right now," he said. "As long as I continue working, there's no real problems. But after that ends, it's going to be pretty slim pickings."

What keeps him going, he said, is his determination to care for Marie and Melody, Marie's granddaughter. The girl was abandoned in infancy by Marie's daughter and her ex-husband.

He teases the girl with savage affection. She said he's teaching her to drive. "I'm teachin' you to be a nerd," he sneered at her.

It troubles him to think that, when Melody is ready for college in a year and a half, he might be unable to send her. But he said he can't keep plugging away 15 hours a day. "I'm just not physically capable of it anymore."

I never asked Bob Johnson the question that echoed silently from the walls of the Marine archive as I scrolled through the record of his desertion and imprisonment: *Why* was his life the way it was?

But he gave me this fragment of an answer:

He was close to his parents but never associated with the rest of his family. "I've spent most of my life alone. And I think a lot. And I've tried to figure out some of these things. And I guess it stems mostly from the horrendous years in my early youth, during this Depression era, when everybody lived in a desperate sort of existence."

A few days before Halloween, I drove southeast to the desolate villages where he grew up—Whitt, Perrin, Newcastle—and to the larger towns, Vernon and Graham, where his divorced parents died.

Vida Mae Dozier, his oldest sister, and her husband, Roger, live in Vernon. Next to their house is a brick shed in which Vida Mae stored her mother's things after Ruby Johnson died in 1986.

Vida Mae said Bob's only real bond was to his mother. She said he always seemed to want the better things, "and we did well to have the bare necessities."

She remembers Ruby had pictures of me as an infant that my mother mailed. They would have been in the shed, but thieves cleaned it out. Presumably, the thieves scattered the photos to the prairie wind.

Vida Mae said her father, Ben Loyd Johnson, left her mother after Bob was grown. Ruby Johnson remarried six times. Vida Mae said she was embarrassed "when all these husbands started bobbing up on the scene.... It seemed kind of frivolous."

Bob's only other living sister, Gay Hicks of Iowa Park, Texas, said she heard of my birth when she was about 10. She remembered my mother's name was Martha.

Neither sister had seen Bob since their mother died.

I talked to Bob Johnson's niece Theresa Massat, who spent years compiling a Johnson family history. From it, I learned that two of Bob's sisters, Imogene and Jo Ella, had killed themselves.

"I think because my family was so fractured, that's one reason I clung to this," Theresa said.

Each in our own way, we were searching for the pieces that, fit together, would make it all make sense. But, traveling through that haunted landscape, I realized I didn't have to make sense of it.

The ghosts here were powerless to do me harm. A bastion of love erected long ago would keep them forever at bay.

I have a letter from my mother to her parents. It was obviously written soon after my birth, but it's dated simply "Sunday night."

In it, she said she'd heard from Bob that week, and learned he was being discharged but was too sick to work. That meant she'd probably have to go back to work herself, she said.

"But I don't feel a bit sorry for myself. I wouldn't go back to a year ago and be without Michael for anything. He is far more than I ever had before to make life worth living."

A few days before she died, as she lay in agony in the porch room where she gave me her first hard advice, she gave me her last.

All those years before, she'd told me never to do what Bob Johnson did to her. This time, she seemed to voice a lesson she'd learned since then.

"Don't be bitter, son."

Bob Johnson gave me life. He did me no real harm, and when I asked him for the truth, he told me as much of it as he could bear to tell.

That seems enough to ask of a father.

I got back to Bob and Marie's the day before Halloween. Hereford had a home football game that night, and the marching band would wear Halloween costumes. Melody was done up as a fetching witch.

I listened to Bob's tales of road mishaps and animals he'd loved—the black poodle, a basset hound he'd brought back from hypothermia with his own body heat, a big yellow cat he slept with in his cab so it wouldn't get lonely—as the local TV cable channel broadcast the audio of the game behind a static station logo and scrolling weather report.

Hereford was up 34-0, and the reserves were in. A boy named Perales caught his first pass ever and ran 39 yards to the end zone, slaying the ghost of the touchdown he never scored.

"Turn out the lights, the party's over," an announcer sang. "Turn out the lights, all good things must end."

Next day, our last, Bob got home early. I was taking him and Marie to dinner at their favorite steak house. Melody was at a lock-in party at a church.

When Marie opened the door to some trick-or-treaters, Pokey, Bob's white poodle, dashed out and made a quick tour of neighbors' lawns. Bob trolled for the dog in his battered Toyota. When the dog jumped in, he rewarded it with a drive around the block.

He put on a new pair of running shoes with Velcro straps. "In honor of the occasion," he said. As we headed out, he pulled on a jean jacket, grinned impishly and said, "This is my evening attire."

The waitresses were all in costume. Ghouls hurried along the aisle as Marie, a former waitress, told of Bob's reputation as a tightwad with the waitresses in Dalhart. When they saw him coming, they'd say, "Oh, no, here comes 35 cents."

He said he and Marie visited his mother the last Christmas she was alive. His mother had cooked the dinner. It was a good Christmas.

In his mother's eyes, he said, he could do no wrong.

I left him sitting in his living room with a cigarette in his hand and the little white dog in his lap.

Marie gave me the weather report. A norther was howling down through Dalhart, gusting to 60 mph, heading for Hereford.

Blowing hard enough to drive the last ghosts of October out across the plains, until they fray to nothingness among the green shoots of winter wheat.

EPILOGUE

Bob Johnson told me his three other sons had gone to school in Hawthorne, California. I've confirmed that the oldest one graduated from high school there. I've gotten no leads on the whereabouts of any of the three.

I got a Christmas card from Bob. It said, "To Son and His Wife." Vida Mae told me she and Gay got Christmas cards from him too. She said she didn't remember ever getting one from him before.

I called Bob on Christmas Day. He said he was taking three days off and sleeping a lot.

He wanted to know about our new house in Louisville, and whether it was on high ground. He wanted to know if we could see the river from there.

Observations and questions

1) This last part begins with an anecdotal lead. Johnson lies injured in the cold. Then,

> I like to think that, as he lay there, my mother's ghost came to him from deep within the frozen earth.
>
> "Bob," she whispered to him. "You've got to wake up, or you'll die here.
>
> "I forgive you, if that's what's bothering you. You gave me a life that meant more to me than my own. Let me give you back yours."

Jennings calls this venture into ghostly voices in the head purely fictional. Does he introduce it adequately to avoid misleading the reader? Try different ways of framing the passage.

2) The father's chronology continues. Study how Jennings interweaves viewpoints from outside the father's account to enrich the readers' understanding.

3) In this section, the author finally finds the worthy father he has searched for by redefining worthiness. How does Jennings keep readers from seeing this real-life compromise as rationalization or simply giving up?

4) This piece has four endings:
  A. "...would keep them forever at bay."
  B. "That seems enough to ask of a father."
  C. "...among the green shoots of winter wheat."
  D. "...if we could see the river from there."

Think about the effects of multiple endings on the readers. We could say they confuse readers, that so complex a series needs all the strands knit up, that hard emotional issues can't have simple endings, etc. Experiment with stopping the story and series with each of the endings above. What different effects do you achieve?

5) This series has struck something deep in many readers. What and why? And why do we in newspapers so seldom strike our readers so deeply?

A conversation with
Mike Jennings

DON FRY: Excuse this question, but aren't you a little old for the schools beat?

MIKE JENNINGS: I got assigned to cover schools when I was in Birmingham. It was against my desire at the time, but I've been doing it ever since. I do a pretty good job, I guess, and that has been the incentive for editors to keep me on the beat.

I personally think schools is the most important beat, because it's about children, money, and the future. Let me repeat that so no one will miss it: THE MOST IMPORTANT BEAT IN A NEWSPAPER IS EDUCATION.

Well, *The Courier-Journal* has a strong, long history of treating schools as an important beat. People covering education here have typically not been younger reporters, so in *Courier-Journal* terms, I'm not an anomaly. But I would prefer to go on to something else now. I don't want to spend the rest of my career as an education writer.

No one should. I'll put that message to your editors in the book, right here.

Thanks.

Was this series your idea?

Yes. It started just as a thought that grew until it became nearly an obsession. I had never really thought at all, to the best of my recollection,

---

[Editor's Note: I have heavily edited and rearranged this conversation for brevity and clarity, and recomposed the questions.]

about trying to track down my natural father. Some time after my mother died in the summer of 1987, I began to ruminate upon the possibility of trying to find him. Then I came into some money from a land transaction, and I was able to quit my job with *The Birmingham News*. I did some free-lance work, and while I looked for a new newspaper job, I started the search for my natural father.

So you originated this as a free-lancer?

Well, at that time, I had no idea of writing about it, I just wanted to try to find this guy. It was quite late in the game that I conceived the idea of actually writing and publishing it.

I proceeded in what I think was a reasonably well-thought-out fashion. The series spells out the most important parts, but there were a number of false trails that I did not report. There was a lot of blundering about.

Why did you want to find your father?

Well, if you don't know who one or the other of your natural parents is, you feel that's something every person has a right to know. And, given that I had some time to do this, and there was no longer anyone still living who could be hurt by it, I just thought that this was something I wanted to do, and it made sense to do.

There were two ancillary reasons, one being that, as I approached middle age, I found pieces of my anatomy starting to go wrong, and you start to think upon mortality and upon the fact that you might have inherited something that will catch up with you. And another part was just journalistic pride. Even though I've never been designated as an investigative reporter, I take some pride in my investigative skills. And it was a real challenge to test my gumshoe abilities.

Had you found him before you decided to write this story?

No. Sometime during 1992, I began to think of writing it as I began to sense I was nearing the end of my search, particularly after I got the documents from the National Personnel Records Center. That pretty well assured me that if I kept at it, I could track him down.

I proposed it to an editor I felt would be receptive to this kind of idea, in August of '92. And just a few days after that, I actually spoke to Bob Johnson for the first time.

So you tried to sell this idea to an editor before you knew the ending?

Yeah. I told him I was on the verge of finding this guy, and he was immediately taken by the idea. I have to say with great gratitude that I got nothing but encouragement and understanding from the editors at *The Courier-Journal* about this whole project. I thought that some of them would feel this was not a news story at all, that it was too personal and too special for a newspaper, but none of them took that position.

What section did you sell it to?

Well, I approached Hunt Helm, the metro editor, which is our fancy new term for city editor.

Where did it run?

It ran in the A-Section, front page, with a jump each day.

Was that decision made before it was written?

No. I told Hunt I didn't expect them to commit to publish something this off-the-wall before they had seen it. I just wanted some indication that they were willing to consider it for publication, and he said, "By all means." He talked it over with the managing editor and some other editors. But the decision to publish it wasn't made until I started submitting the parts of the series.

After you had done the reporting, how did you plan this story?

Well, I was worried, maybe unduly so, that this story would be too far outside the bounds of what people read in a newspaper. Unless I shaped it very carefully and did my best to make it compelling and interesting to read, the editors might dismiss it out of hand, and if they didn't, readers might be turned off by it, or bored by it, or think it was not worth their while. So my first priority was to make it interesting, to make it readable, and to organize it in a way that matched as closely as possible the kind of thing newspapers usually do. So I thought in terms of a several-part series, no part of which would run longer than what *The Courier-Journal* usually allows in a series, which is 30 to 40 inches. So I thought in terms of making it compelling, and of organizing it in readable chunks.

When did you start writing it?

In November. I had gone to Texas in late October, and I spent a lot of time over the next couple of weeks typing up just about everything and organizing. I transcribed the information off the muster rolls, written in a kind of military shorthand, and I had to translate some of that using a military manual, and at one point, calling up a Marine source to ask for help in determining what some of this terminology meant.

And how did you organize all those notes?

In chronological form. I taped all my conversations with Bob Johnson, and I transcribed all those word for word. I did a chronology of his Marine career, a transcription of his entries in the muster rolls, and all of the observations that I had made while I was in Texas.

Did you decide from the beginning on a five-part series?

No. I was aiming for as short a handling as I could without doing violence to the story. If I could do that in a 3-part or 4-part series, I would have. I didn't have any idea when I started writing the first part, how many parts I would end up writing. I wrote until I was somewhere in the 30- to 40-inch range, and starting looking for a transition point. And when I found that transition point, I would break off that piece and go on to the next. But I didn't know it was going to be a five-part series until somewhere in the middle of the writing process.

How long did it take you to write the whole thing?

Not that long. Even though the transcription of all of that source material was a grueling process, it paid off because I had everything I needed in organized form close at hand, and I knew where to look for the pieces. The writing took from late November until a few days before Christmas. I would say that the total writing time was between four and six days.

That doesn't add up.

I would write a draft, or a piece of the story, and then do other things on my beat for a few days. During that time, I would go back to what I had originally written and massage it. I submitted to Hunt Helm, the editor I was working with, as many as two or three drafts of each story. So the first drafts I probably did in as little as four days, but the rewriting process probably consumed more like two weeks.

Did you find it hard to write?

It was surprisingly easy until I got down toward the end. The last two parts were harder
because I had been saving some things, some
observations and, I guess more importantly,
what I felt about them, until I found the right
place to put them. And as I got down toward
the end, I realized I either had to use them
there, or let them go and not use them at all.
Plus, I was working in a deadline situation, so
I had to finish up the last two pieces in about
two or three days.

Were you edited much?

No, it wasn't. Very lightly.

How did it run?

It started December 27 and ended the last day
of the year, and every day, it started on 1A and
jumped.

With art?

Yes. I had taken photos in Texas, and the paper
did a splendid job of handling them; they also
did a map and a logo that ran with each day's
part.

What was the response?

Well, I didn't know at first, because we were on
Christmas vacation in Minnesota when it ran.

**Your great masterpiece runs, and you're not
even in the state!**

Well, our editor, David Hawpe, called while we
were in Minnesota, and said that the response to
the series had been between two extremes: great
enthusiasm and questioning why in the world we
were putting such tripe in the newspaper. [Don
laughs; Mike doesn't.] And I had expected the
latter, but I was glad to hear the former.

Did *you* like it?

Given the terms I had to work with, and that
this had to be published in a newspaper, yes, I
was satisfied, or as close to being satisfied as
I'm probably going to get from that large an
undertaking. But I felt that in making it good
for publication in a newspaper, I did some violence, and I couldn't have avoided doing that
to the truth of the situation and what I felt
about it.

So turn it into a book.

I've thought of that. Yes.

**Let's talk about part one. Where do you think
the lead ends?**

I think it ends after "...plains of north Texas."

**Eight paragraphs is an awfully long lead for a
story! [Don laughs; Mike doesn't.]**

Yes. Well..., I was trying to put something up
front that would dramatize the whole situation
in as compelling a way as I could and make it
concrete, without straying outside the facts. I
took some care to do some scene painting, and
to evoke an air of mystery.

**All right. Why did you start here with your fa-
ther at the end of the war?**

Well, because that was the most compelling image I could come up with, and also because
that's where I started. That's all I knew of him:
He had been a Marine. He had been at Camp
Lejeune. He had come briefly into my mother's
life and then disappeared, fate dropping him
down in eastern North Carolina where my
mother happened to be about to go to work at
a school.

And you decided not to tell readers for a while that this was your father?

Yes.

Yes, but readers aren't used to puzzles at the top; they're used to being told things right away.

Well, I wanted it to be a mystery, and I tried to make that explicit not too far into the story by saying this is a mystery story. There were a lot of things that I didn't know until very late in the process, and I wanted the stories to replicate in some fashion the sense of not knowing, and very much needing and wanting to know, that I had felt as I went through this search.

Part one ends in a cliffhanger: "A year and a half after she died, I decided I would track my ghost to its lair, I would find what substance lay behind its phantom shape.

"The man I had good cause to call my true father had died in 1980. Finding Robert Johnson, I thought, could harm no one still living.

"There were two people still alive whom I was neglecting to count. I was one of them.

"I had not yet met the other, at least not in the flesh."
Was that passage hard to write?

Yes. Well, that first piece wrote itself very easily and very quickly, and...

What do you mean by "wrote itself"?

I had written it pretty much in my head before I typed it out.

Had you been composing this in your head for a while?

Yes.

Do you normally write in your head?

No. But I had been thinking, even before I met Bob Johnson, about the pieces of this story, and I knew some of the things, some paragraphs, certainly some episodes, that I wanted in there. I didn't know what order they would fall into, but by the time I started writing, I pretty much knew how this first part would read, and it was almost just a matter of typing it out.

I do most of my writing in my head. In the shower, while driving, and then I dictate to my computer.

I can't cover a meeting and write the story in my head on the way back to the office. Some people can do that, and I envy them, but I'm not one of them. But if I can ruminate on something over a period, I can do that.

Did you use the same headline all five days: "The Search for My Father"?

Yes.

Did you write that?

No. Someone had suggested "The Search for My Dad," and Hunt, knowing how I felt about both my natural and my adoptive father, immediately said, "No, that won't do. He doesn't regard this guy as his *dad*." So he saw to it that it was changed to "Father."

Treasure such a sensitive editor! Where does the lead end in part two?

After paragraph four: "...quite true."

Tricky lead.

Well, I did struggle with that lead. I was trying to come up with some concrete image that would convey the sense of blind groping through so much of this process. I knew so little about this guy, and as I turned up facts, they were not what I expected, and they seemed to lead in no very definitive direction.

The raw past is by definition disorganized.

Yes. The past, as we read about it in history books, or as it's related to us by our parents or older people generally, bears scant relation to what we're likely to find if we actually go burrowing back and sifting the evidence on our own. There's a lot of stuff that gets edited out because it's too painful.

Did you know that before this search?

Well, as a process of just having lived long enough, the biography that any 46-year-old man would tell his children is not going to include all of the significant episodes of his life. I was searching for the dark side of the man, and that's a lot like blundering around in a cave and coming across things that aren't too savory, as would be true in the case of most men.

Let's take a look at paragraph 20: "I came across two Robert Johnsons and two John Johnsons before hitting on Pvt. James R. Johnson, service number 297916. He was a light antiaircraft gun crewman in Company B, 1st Battalion, 1st Marines, 1st Marine Division, stationed in Tientsin, China. A footnote said that on July 24th, the day after my birth, Pvt. Johnson left Tientsin for discharge in the United States."
Strikingly out of tone with the prose around it.

Yes. Well, it was striking at the time. After all this blundering around, here was something I could put my hands on.

You frame the passage, starting, "Within four hours, I found my father," followed by all this

Marine Corps lingo, and then closing the frame with this deadpan comment: "The Marines are meticulous record-keepers."

They are.

This part has two chronologies. One starts in paragraph five ("In the winter of 1989..."), the other in paragraph 32 ("He enlisted in Los Angeles in September 1940."). You organize the whole piece around these chronologies. Chronology is rare in newswriting, unfortunately.

Well, that was one of the reasons I feared people might be turned off if it fell into a pattern of "and next this happened, and after that this happened," that if I let that go on too long, it would certainly turn people off. So I was trying hard to break up the chronological unwinding with things that would bring it to life.

Chronologies are lists, very efficient for getting readers through a lot of material in a hurry, and they also tend to orient the reader.

Well, the preliminary work helped me here because I had put together a careful chronology, and I just lifted chunks out of my notes into the stories.

Did you have a master chronology somewhere?

Yes.

There are essentially two chronologies. One is the chronology of *his life,* and the other is the chronology of *your search.* Were those kept separate?

Yes.

Part two ends with another cliffhanger: "It occurred to me that I could quietly close the book on Robert Johnson. I knew enough, I thought.

Perhaps too much.

"There were two problems with that idea. One was that I wasn't sure that the James R. Johnson in the muster rolls was who I thought he was. The other was that cutting short my search would not make my father's ghost go away. It would be right there in my footsteps, treading closer behind me than ever, until I turned and looked it in the face."

That was designed as a cliffhanger, and, in fact, after I had looked back over the whole series, I feared that I had made the cliffhangers at the ends of parts one and two too much in the same pattern, because both of them were a one-two punch. But, yes, I was quite cynical in designing an ending for each of these pieces that would make the reader want to turn to the next piece. And again, this was largely out of my fear that unless I really carefully fashioned this to make people want to go on, they wouldn't.

That's not cynicism; that's what compelling writing means.

They might not be compelling enough.

That one is. And there's another story going on here: the evolution of your thought and emotion. Certainly this passage marks a turning point where you had to make a decision.

Yes.

Were you ever afraid of what you'd find?

Yes. I constantly had a queasy, sinking feeling about what I would find. But after having the really sinking feeling of finding what I found in the muster rolls, I concluded that whatever I found after that couldn't be any worse....

An axe murderer maybe....

...unless this guy turned out to be an axe murderer. I concluded that I really had nothing to lose by going on.

Part three starts flying right into the narrative of the search, no lead at all, no framing.

I assume that anybody who has made it this far has read parts one and two, and so I'm making it a continuous narrative without any orientation to the whole subject.

Paragraph 12 is very, very important, because this is where you and your father get tied together: "The first page bore Robert Johnson's enlistment photograph. That just about killed off any doubt. It could have been my own photo at the same age."

When I got that envelope from St. Louis, it was almost like looking in a mirror, not a mirror at the age I am now, but at the age of 25 or so. This could have been me. There are a lot of Robert Johnsons out there, and a lot of Robert Johnsons during World War II, and probably some, more than one, at Camp Lejeune. And so I had kept open the possibility that this guy I was tracking was somebody else. But that sealed the case.

A great moment, in your life and in this story. This part ends with a long conversation, mostly in direct quotations. First of all, how did you get that?

I taped it. This was the day I found out where he was, and his wife called me after she found out that I was trying to get in touch with this guy. I didn't know how I would be received, whether he would be hostile, or this might be my only opportunity ever to talk to the guy. So I didn't want to miss the opportunity of at least hearing what his voice sounded like.

Was the taping legal?

Unlike Florida, where you have to inform people you're taping over the phone, there is no such law in Kentucky.

Right. Did he know about the taping?

I didn't tell him I was taping at that point. When I actually met him, I had the tape recorder out there in full view, and he had no objection.

Yes. You might have scared him to death if you told him you were taping the first time.

Well, I assume so. And when it came time to write this, I was very glad that I had that tape, so that I could get that verbatim. I edited a few things out, but the thread of the conversation was just as the story presents it.

Journalists very seldom capture real speech. We usually clean it up a lot, mostly by omission. But this sounds real.

That conversation was mostly as I wrote it, except leaving out some "uhs" and a very few lines. The portion I used was pretty much continuous, but this is not the entire conversation. We talked about other things, but I didn't heavily edit the part I actually used.

It doesn't sound like you edited much at all, except to leave out fillers.

Yes.

By leaving out a lot of the sentences, I think you've made it quite spare, which it needs to be at this point.

Yes.

Particularly this paragraph: "Very quietly he said, 'I see.' He cleared his throat. 'Now, I think I know what the relationship is.'" You

**convey emotion from outward signs only. You
don't look inside his head. Very spare.**

Well, that was right there on the tape; I didn't
have to search around or cook any of that out.

It's kind of bare country speech.

He's a kind of bare country guy. He's really a
very interesting conversationalist. He's not
well-educated, but he's an intelligent man, and
he's fun to talk to.

Later on, he's very articulate.

He is very articulate.

In a plain kind of way.

He is very articulate.

**Early in part four, you look across real and
symbolic landscapes: "I thought of how a
slight tilt of destiny's wheel might have allotted
me some Bob Johnson other than the one who
shirked his war, deceived a school teacher, went
to China, and had his hollow-eyed photograph
taken there, and 46 years later spoke to me in a
voice that sounded as dust-scoured as the arid
Texas plains when I ran him to earth."
You tend to look across landscapes like that
at key moments in your story.**

You can see a long way in Texas.

Yes, into the emotions.

Yes. And traveling out there from Louisville,
where the horizon is landlocked, it..., you feel
kind of bare and naked out there, particularly
at that time of year, getting on toward winter.
And I found I couldn't leave the landscape out
of it because it had a lot to do with how I ended
up feeling about the whole experience.

And then finally, you meet: "I stepped up on a latticed metal running board and looked in at the averted, weathered face with its high, tilted cheekbones, narrow moustache and outsized ears. His flattened nose had whorled edges, like those on a Mayan bust. Compared to his compact torso, his dungaree-clad shanks looked astonishing long and spindle-thin. His belt was lined with little bronze medallions and fastened with a rectangular white buckle."

Was that description done from memory, or did you go away and write down notes?

Well, that was largely reconstructed, based on what I saw of him over the next week. Actually I didn't get to see that much of him; it was just that night and the next day, and then two evenings at the end of my stay there. His facial features registered immediately, but the little bronze medallions, all of that, were not something I could have reconstructed in that way if I had seen him on that occasion and never again. But seeing him and confirming those details over the rest of my stay there, and knowing that I had seen all of that, and feeling that I had noticed it all at some level when I first stepped up there and got my first good look at him, I felt I was warranted in putting that all into that scene.

Sure....

But I do not have mental photographic capacity that would have enabled me to reconstruct that description in that detail if I had stepped down from that running board and never seen him again.

It's a very striking description, because we've had little bits of him before in photographs, and suddenly, we come face to face with the ghost, and we get him full blast. And in a way, that's what we've been wanting, isn't it? [Long pause] But I guess you can't read this as a

reader, can you?

No. I can't read it as a reader.

Well, I'm the reader, and I'll tell you that that's what I've been waiting for. I want to meet this man, this ghost, face to face, and I want to know all of what he looks like.

Well, I'm glad you feel that way, because that's exactly how I felt at that time.

Then you start chronology all over again. The whole series of chronologies keeps getting re-constructed and re-reconstructed, and here he is telling it himself, so we're at the source, and we get a lot of him.

Yes.

This was taped?

Yes. This was taped. Presenting the spare chronology that the military records had laid out for me, and then the fleshed-out chronology once I had met him, and then he was able to speak in his own voice, all that meant going over much of the same ground. I was aware of the risks of unnecessary duplication there, but I felt I had to, because it had so much to do with the experience. With this man I knew only from bits and pieces of documentary evidence, all I had was two dimensions, if that. And meeting him, suddenly, everything sprang into..., into..., into three dimensions and into color. And I wanted to try to convey the contrast between the two.

Well, it's a very rich telling, and it's very bare because he's telling it with very little quoting. His version just zooms right along.

Yes.

At the end of part four, you break right off in the middle of his narrative. Talk about a cliffhanger!

Well, that was again one of those cases of coming down to 40 inches and knowing that I had better get the hell out of there, or I'd hear from my editors. But in that moment he's describing there, he decided that the best thing that he could do for my mother was to stay out of her life. That was obviously a turning point for everybody involved. There it was decided that I would never meet this guy unless I took the initiative. So when I found that, I just slapped it in the story at that point.

Then part five can start with this wonderful anecdote of nearly freezing to death, no lead or anything, straight to this strange scenario that starts in paragraph three: "I like to think that, as he lay there, my mother's ghost came to him from deep within the frozen earth.

"'Bob,' she whispered to him. 'You've got to wake up, or you'll die here.'

"'I forgive you, if that's what's bothering you. You gave me a life that meant more to me than my own. Let me give you back yours.'"
You're reading the mind of your dead mother! [Don laughs; Mike doesn't.]

I understand that. Well, that's the only pure fiction except for the dream in part one, and I can't quite decide whether I'm actually remembering that first dream from childhood or fabricating it. I just flat don't know. The story needed it right there, and I think that a careful reader can assimilate that without drawing back and saying, "What is he doing here? He's writing a factual story, and suddenly ghosts are talking in it." I hope it's clear that this is a sidestep into fiction to capture an emotional dimension that belongs there, and nothing more than that.

You signal clearly: "I like to think that...." But it's still a daring touch. Did you debate that?

54

Yes. I debated it, but not very long, because I was writing on deadline at that point.

Did you debate it with the editors?

No. I just went ahead and put it in to see how they'd react, and they took no issue with it.

On the text in front of you, draw lines as follows:
1. After "...would keep them forever at bay."
2. After "That seems enough to ask of a father."
3. Between "...winter wheat." and "Epilogue."
4. And then at the end.
This piece has four endings. See?

Yes. You're right. Yes. The story, and the series, operated on several levels, the first being my lifelong search for this ghost. When I finally caught up with it, there was no substance to it at all, and it would vanish and never haunt me again. That level of the story came to an end at the first line.

"Forever at bay"?

Yes. And then I had to deal on a different level with a real man, not a ghost, but a man I had finally found. I had to decide how I was going to feel for the rest of my life about this real individual. And that resolution is reached at the second line.

"Enough to ask of a father."

Yes. And then this trip that came to its end on Halloween night in west Texas, this quest in space and time, was another level on which the story operated, and I tried to bring that to a conclusion at the third line.

"Winter wheat."

Yes. Our deputy managing editor, Rochelle Riley, suggested the epilogue. So I penciled that

one out in Minnesota. And it has to do with
what happened since I left Texas. And I'm glad
she made that suggestion; it seems to fit.

**We're at the end of the story, of the stor*ies*. I
want to ask you a hard question, and I don't
want you to misinterpret it as hostile, or even
skeptical.**

All right.

**I'm talking about the whole thing, all five
parts. Is this story true?**

Yes, with the exception of the two passages I
mentioned: the one dream I'm not completely
sure I ever really dreamed or just made up, and
the one clear case of fictionalizing. But everything else is absolutely accurate insofar as I
could make it.

I'm not asking about accuracy. Is it *true*?

Yes. It's all true. I have no hesitation about
that. Well..., it's as true as I could make it writing for a newspaper and finally meeting a
deadline.
    In the last piece, I did a gimmicky sort of
thing to help the story wind down, that omit-
ted one of the rough corners of truth, or bev-
eled that corner off in a way that really was
misleading. I said, "A bastion of love erected
long ago would keep them forever at bay." If
there is anything in the whole series that I liked
least, because I feel it was fabricated rather
than the true reflection of what I experienced
and felt, I guess that transition is it.
    I'm trying to say there that the love my
mother surrounded me with was sufficient for
all of my life to protect me from any harm,
from what my father did, or the circumstances
of his family history, which are pretty tragic,
but I couldn't get into them in any detail in this
story. And I'm uneasy with that transition be-

cause it ties things up too neatly. I don't really feel all that secure about my relationship with this guy. Life isn't that neat, and it's a bit phony to suggest that it can be, or that I felt that it was. But I sensed that 40-inch limit approaching, and I had to cut things off a little bit more sharply than I might otherwise have done.

But, yes, it's not the whole truth, but it is true.

You know, since the announcement came out about this prize and what the stories are about, people keep asking me for copies of your series. They think your story will have resonance in their lives, so you've touched a nerve.

That's interesting, but I did not imagine it would be taken in that way. I'm delighted that it resonates for them, and not just for adoptees.

One of our photographers passed me in the newsroom and said that, as a man who was raised by his mother, "I just want to thank you for writing that story."

Me too.

Richard O'Mara

Finalist, Non-Deadline Writing

Richard O'Mara, the *Sun*'s London correspondent since 1991, covers Europe and sometimes Africa. He worked at *The Buenos Aires Herald* before coming to Baltimore. There he wrote editorials, edited the weekly Perspective section, and served as foreign editor for 12 years. Last year in Somalia, he saw death close up.

The headline of this piece captures his strategy perfectly: "Awakening the World to Action: Try Guilt." O'Mara contrasts Western thinking about former Yugoslavia, dominated by heroic notions of war, against reductive notions of famine in Somalia. Events catch up with us; eight months later (April 1993), we've saved Somalia and lost Yugoslavia.

Awakening the world to action: Try guilt

AUGUST 23, 1992

MOGADISHU, Somalia—In 1952, a Brazilian nutritionist named Josue de Castro published a book called *The Geography of Hunger.*

In it, Mr. de Castro noted that though hunger "had unquestionably been the most potent source of social misfortunes...our civilization has kept its eyes averted, afraid to face the sad reality. War has always been loudly discussed. Hymns and poems have been written to celebrate its glorious virtue.... Thus, while war became a leitmotif of Western thought, hunger remained only a vulgar sensation, the repercussions of which were not supposed to emerge from the realm of the subconscious. The conscious mind, with ostentatious disdain, denied its existence."

Forty years later, that strange aversion prevails.

Men are drawn to war; their minds are obsessed with it, possibly because it holds the potential for heroism. Hunger runs rampant, and the world turns away. There are no flags associated with it, no summons to glory.

In Somalia today, there is a massive famine. It is the offspring of a civil war of about four years duration. But the famine is the major factor today; the war is secondary as an agent of death.

More than a year into this extraordinary tragedy, the Western world has finally been embarrassed into attention. The capacity for indifference toward Somalia seemed especially callous when compared with the concern so evident in every Western capital over the strife in the former country of Yugoslavia. These two conflicts have divided the world once again along its major fault line—between the rich and the poor nations.

Boutros Boutros-Ghali, the secretary-general of the United Nations, has undiplomatically called attention to the discrepancy.

Reflecting Third World sentiment, Mr. Boutros-Ghali declared the Balkans conflict to be the "rich man's war." He has denounced the Security Council for its obsession with the Balkan bloodletting, to the neglect of what James Kunder, in the State Department's Office of Disaster Assistance, declared to be "the world's worse humanitarian crisis."

The secretary-general, an Egyptian diplomat of many years' experience, was accused of lacking diplomacy.

"He is losing his job because he is saying this," says Nuruddin Farah, a Somali novelist. "The European world does not like being told it is racist."

There may indeed be racism involved in this. All races have a natural impulse toward their own kind. But probably this other factor is at work as well, what Mr. de Castro called "the hidden motives that have led our culture to abstain from dealing with the problem of hunger."

What are these motives? Why does this happen?

Possibly famine is so difficult to confront because it is the ultimate failure of civilization. Wars are a lesser breakdown of civilization—and not always that, for some wars are controlled and do not rip apart the fabric of social and economic life. Wars have been institutionalized, rationalized; the conduct of them is overlaid with rules.

Armies are invested with tradition and legitimate purpose. People who organize and conduct wars are honored, respected as professionals. Nothing else generates the passion of patriotism among people as much as war. For no other activity are medals and honors dispensed so plentifully as for making war.

Usually the functions of life go on during a war. Famine annihilates all. Its effects are more extensive; the biological and social consequences perpetuate themselves. The loss of life from a war is made up again. The survivors of great famines are broken for all their lives; their children inherit the frailty of their parents. They are a weight that retards the recovery of the people as a whole.

Famines are daunting, mysterious and almost always the product of human inadvertence. Nature makes droughts and floods; men make famines. They are the sign that politics has failed, political organization has collapsed, for famine is predictable. The Romans and civilizations before them understood that so they built granaries and storehouses, for food to carry them through times of natural difficulty.

But it is a mistake to believe famine yields no heroes.

Currently in Somalia, there are more heroes than there are in all the Balkan states put together. Among them are the Somali doctors, many of them Western-trained, who might today be safe in Sweden or Germany, or even Kenya. Instead they staff the hospitals of Mogadishu, stitching up the men brought in from the spasmodic fighting that goes on in this hell of a city. They mend the children shot or blasted by shell fire, crippled by mines.

They are assisted by Somali nurses, who because of their sex are always at risk of being raped. The nurses are soft, gentle, sad, feminine and determined to work until they drop. And then they get up again.

There are heroes in the bush towns like Bardera, the medical workers with the United Nations Children's Fund who flew to that devastated village with the intention of feeding and giving medicine only to distressed children.

Once arrived they were almost overwhelmed by the thousands of people streaming in from the scrubland, people no longer possessed of minds that think, but driven by the first and most basic animal instinct: to eat.

The refugees are beaten back from the gates of the compound by men with guns and sticks, determined to keep some order in the process of rescue.

But the means are so scant. Dr. Ayub Sheik Yerow stands in the dusty compound, his ebony face glistening. He pleads with some journalists, flown in for an hour or two, to tell the world that he needs food in Bardera, that Somalia needs food right away.

As if the world doesn't know.

The only semblance of organization in Somalia has been brought by foreigners, most of them from the Western relief agencies, but not all: the Red Crescent is active. The so-called nongovernmental organizations, or NGOs, such as Save the Children, Swedrelief, Irish Concern, Catholic Relief Services, the Lutheran church's group, operate efficiently and move quickly because of their small size. They criticize the larger organizations connected to the United Nations for their torpid response to the growing crisis.

But the United Nations, in the end, is more essential. It will provide the benign bureaucracy that will make the overall effort work.

"Only the United Nations can take over an entire country," said E. Scott Osborne of Baltimore-based Catholic Relief Services. "Only they can provide the structure. They have the planes, the trucks, everything that is needed."

A Canadian doctor named Pete, who declines to give his last name, speaks only about the work before him and doesn't have much time to reveal any opinions about the "situation."

Maybe he doesn't have any. If not, that doesn't reflect a personal shallowness so much as a personal strategy, a decision to allow no distractions into his mind. Besides, who can contemplate the madness of Somalia for very long without deciding to leave?

For that reason many of the relief workers go around not unthinking, but rather dealing with the detail of their work, suspending their instincts to contemplate this predicament.

A young Irish nurse encountered in squalid Baidoa is keenly aware that publicity will help her obtain the food and medicines her team needs. Why else would she give time to reporters? Reporters don't give shots, save lives.

It is a rational calculation; it worked in Ethiopia. Awaken the world's conscience. Appeal in any way possible. Try guilt. Try anything.

None of these people seems at all vainglorious or self-seeking. They act the way we think heroes should act: modestly, perfunctorily, trying to get the job done. Men like Arthur Klauck, the unshaven German with the United Nations Development Program. He's trying to keep the water clean, drinkable. He continues his work, and his hand is never far from a gun.

Guilt is not a factor at the scene, though it may be among people far removed from here in the comfortable countries of North America and Europe, who may suspect that they have much because these people have so little.

Whether there is a connection between one country's prosperity and another's destitution is something political scientists can argue over. Here, all that matters is what is happening in front of them.

Who has time to think about motives, altruistic, self-serving or whatever kind? There's just too much work to do, and too little time.

The Providence Journal

Randall Richard

Finalist, Non-Deadline Writing

Joel Rawson, deputy executive editor of *The Providence Journal,* calls his reporters "news carnivores," and Randall Richard fits that description. In 26 years there, he has covered the city, the state, and the world, investigating everything from drug dealing to adoption markets. He has prizes to match.

Richard's five-part series on "Russia Searching for its Soul" starts with an 18-paragraph lead. But, like everything he writes, those 18 paragraphs grab the readers so fast they never notice the author who guides them through hard thinking. Part one is reprinted here.

Freed from communism, but bound by the past

DECEMBER 13, 1992

ST. PETERSBURG—The curtain separating his bed from the rest of his parents' one-room flat was bone white and thin, a billowing fog in the midnight chill, and Vladimir Ermon could clearly make out the shadows closing in on his father's bear-like silhouette.

The gray men in the long, gray greatcoats had finally come, just as he always knew they would, but in the muted light from the street-lamps of Nevsky Prospekt they were even more terrifying than he had imagined.

Except for his own racing heart and the snow-deadened clang of a trolley from the street below, the room was eerily silent, and for a moment or two Vladimir Ermon was not quite sure if this wasn't just another of his terrible nightmares.

The other children at school all had these nightmares, too, and everyone, it seemed, knew somebody whose nightmare had just come true.

He bolted upright in his bed, gasping for breath, as a dozen flashlights went on at once, blinding his father, roaming shamelessly over his mother's body and darting along the book-shelves that ran from ceiling to floor along the entire length of the flat.

The Iliad was on the kitchen table, still open to the passage his father had been reading to him only a few hours before. Scattered over the rest of the table were sketches of Greek warriors, the ones he'd draw whenever his father read to him from Homer, the ones his father always joked would surely send Leonardo, if ever he saw them, into uncontrollable fits of envy.

Though the flat was only one room, it was cavernous, 40 meters square—a home befitting a hero of the Bolshevik revolution—with a grand view of the grandest street in all of Russia.

The gray men brandished their pistols and barked their orders, but his father stood his ground. He would not be hurried. And when he finally spoke, it was with such authority that even these gray men, Stalin's dreaded secret police, all but snapped to attention.

His father, who had so valiantly fought the Germans in 1914, who had left his native Estonia to help lead Trotsky's Red Army brigades to Bolshevism's final victory, would meet his fate with dignity. But first he would say his goodbys to his son, and Stalin's jackals would have to wait, quietly and respectfully, as he did so.

It was then that Vladimir Ermon knew with a child's certainty what he had to do. There was only one way to stop what was happening, only one way to save his father's life.

And so, with all the strength a 10-year-old could muster, he choked back his sobs and snapped shut his eyes as his father approached.

This frail but precocious only child, who had already reread most of Kipling before his last birthday, decided to will himself back to sleep. He would simply trap those gaunt, gray men in a nightmare from which he would soon awake; and when he did, his father would still be there.

The samovar would already be piping hot and his father would crank up the victrola and listen to Verdi, just as he always did on a Saturday morning. The strong, black tea from Kipling's India would be sweetened with globs of Siberian honey, and then they would all take the trolley down Nevsky Prospekt to the cinema, just as his father had promised the night before.

Even today, 54 years later, Vladimir Ermon closes his eyes as he recounts his father's farewell kiss, as if there was still a slim chance he'd be 10 again when he opened them.

"I think that a foreigner cannot imagine it," he finally says. "To be a specialist, to be competent, to be honest, to be clever, only invited disaster. I cannot find the words to describe the lies and the cruelty. This was a rule of criminals—the victory of the devil—an empire of evil—those were the right words from your President Reagan."

But worse even than what Stalin did, says Ermon, is what the Russian people did to themselves:

"Like children, we all closed our eyes and pretended to be asleep. We lied not only to each other, we lied even to ourselves."

It is this great lie, says Ermon, that the Russian people must now face; and facing it, he warns, with all the shame and the guilt that goes along with it, will be perhaps the most painful of all the painful tasks that lie ahead.

* * *

It was nine years before Vladimir Ermon would see his father again, what little there was that was left of him, in a bleak Stalinist gulag far to the north of the Siberian city of Krasnoyarsk.

Ermon was 19 and had just graduated from secondary school when the authorities finally relented and allowed him to make a pilgrimage that would prove to be the most painful of his life.

All that remained of his father's bear-like frame were the huge bones jutting out at painful angles through a paper-thin coating of jaundiced flesh. His eyes, in deep, gray sockets, seemed to be tunneling toward the back of his head, and the once-authoritative voice was barely audible.

"Did you believe them?" he wheezed—the first words out of his father's mouth.

"No, Papa. Never!"

The answer seemed to put his father at peace.

Above all, even after all the years in the gulag, he wanted his son to know that he was a patriot, a true Leninist and revolutionary, and that it was the Stalinists who had betrayed the revolution, not the millions like him who were being murdered and tortured and exiled.

Perhaps it was that stubborn need to be seen for what he really was, even more than the instinct for survival, that had sustained him during the days that followed his arrest in 1938, at the height of the Stalinist purges.

He had been charged with spying for Latvia, and for three days they had relentlessly beat and tortured him and threatened him with death. But it was only after he had broken the will of his interrogator, after he had gotten his interrogator to admit to the horrible truth, that he finally confessed.

"Yes! Yes! Yes!" his interrogator had burst out in frustration. "We know you are innocent. Do you think we are stupid? If you were a spy we would have already shot you!"

* * *

Seven time zones and 6,000 miles from St. Petersburg, in the tiny Far Eastern settlement of Vodzvizhenka, 68-year-old Nellie Pavlovna, a toothless and slightly mad pensioner, grieves for her father also.

She, too, was only 10 when her father was taken away.

But unlike Ermon's father, whose death was slow and agonizing, General Pavlovna was dead within three weeks.

The legendary commander of Moscow's 408th Regiment, who was wounded 16 times between 1914 and 1917, who had survived the kaiser's shrapnel, czarist bullets and White Army machine gun fire, was shot through the head at Lubiyanka prison on March 20, 1936.

Nellie Pavlovna never got a farewell kiss from her father. She was still at school when they came for him.

In fact, it wasn't until 1956, 20 years after her mother had been arrested as a Trotskyite and placed in a lunatic asylum, that Nellie Pavlovna learned that her father was indeed dead.

And it wasn't until 1962, long after her mother had been released from the asylum only to starve to death during the Nazi siege of Leningrad, that Nellie Pavlovna got her letter, on official government stationery, declaring that her father was innocent after all, that it was all just an unfortunate period in Soviet history.

* * *

Though they have never met, and though they live in vastly different circumstances at opposite ends of the longest railway on earth, Vladimir Ermon and Nellie Pavlovna share far more than childhood pain.

In Russia, painful childhoods are as countless as the Siberian birch trees that separate Vodzvizhenka from St. Petersburg. It is a nation whose peoples are bound by pain—millions killed and exiled and sent to slave labor camps by the czars, millions killed or imprisoned under Stalin, 20 million more killed by the Nazis.

As the children of "enemies of the people," Vladimir Ermon and Nellie Pavlovna, like millions of other Russians, also constantly had to prove themselves in the eyes of the state. Both had to endure one broken promise after another. Both had to live the great lie.

Ermon, who pursued his childhood passion for Kipling and the mysteries of India, is now a distinguished professor of Sanskrit at Leningrad University and the author of several books on the culture, poetry and myths of ancient India.

But it wasn't until Stalin's death, in 1952, that Ermon was even permitted to enroll at Leningrad University, and it wasn't until 1989, four years into Gorbachev's era of glasnost and perestroika, that he was finally considered trustworthy enough, at age 61, to travel outside the then-Soviet Union, on a two-week lecture tour to his beloved India, with his wife and daughter held hostage at home.

Nellie Pavlovna, who followed her father into the military and gained fame under fire during World War II as a communications specialist on the 1st Byelorussian Front, eventually went to work for the KGB, in the very same building, she learned later, where Stalin's secret police had shot her father through the head.

Today, she lives alone and in abject poverty, on a pension of 260 rubles a month (about $2.60 at the current exchange rate). The only thing that keeps her going, she says, is her stubbornness and her dream—a dream to survive just long enough to expose the lies that have haunted her a lifetime, and to complete a project she began nearly 30 years ago, her father's biography.

* * *

It is this legacy of pain, hypocrisy and betrayal —this living of a great lie from one generation to the next—that must first be understood to make any sense of how Russians perceive what is happening in their country today, Ermon says.

His response was in answer to a nagging question.

His foreign guest was troubled, and had told him so.

For six weeks, the guest had been traveling from one end of Russia to the other, from the teeming port city of Vladivostok on the Pacific to the imperial capital of Peter the Great on the Baltic.

He had lived with construction workers, fighter pilots and beekeepers in the Far East, with farmers, students, truck drivers and pensioners in central and western Siberia, with scientists and would-be businessmen in Moscow and St. Petersburg.

He had come to see how things had changed since he had been there last, when Russia was still part of the Soviet Union, when Russians still lived under communism, when church bells were silent, when most citizens dared not criticize their government, at least in public, when they still sent their sons to fight and die in Afghanistan, when they were still barred from some of their own cities—so-called "closed cities" and strategic military sites like Vladivostok and Krasnoyarsk—where even he, a foreigner, was now permitted to freely roam.

Much, indeed, had changed. Farmers were buying their own plots of land. Newspaper headlines screamed about the corruption and mismanagement that had always been there but rarely exposed, at least until the waning days of Gorbachev's era of glasnost. Vendors surrounded virtually every metro in every city from dawn to dusk, hawking everything from curling irons and caviar to Pepsi and pedigree puppies. Nevsky Prospekt and the Arbot were alive with the sounds of trumpets, saxophones and drums, with the music of Bach and Brubeck and Bo Diddley. And the church bells rang at last.

* * *

But much had remained the same, or grown worse. The shelves in the state stores were as empty as ever and the lines outside even longer. Muggings, housebreaks and even armed robberies, almost unheard of in the past, were now commonplace. Alcoholism, drug abuse, homelessness and prostitution, if not far more prevalent, were at least far more obvious. And perhaps most importantly, the sense of frustration, anxiety and disillusionment that had permeated so much of Russian society in the past now seemed to be giving way to an even deeper sense of hopelessness and despair.

At the very time the Russian people were being urged to forget about the past and rejoice in their new freedoms and opportunities, most Russians seemed to speak longingly of the good old days—days when the shops were relatively well-stocked, days when a single kopek could get you across town on the metro, days when you didn't have to dodge the pickpockets and panhandlers on the way home and didn't have to bolt your apartment door when you got here.

* * *

To Vladimir Ermon, who lost his father in those "good old days" and who has devoted much of his life to the study of myths, such attitudes are frightening, but not surprising.

They are grounded, he says, like most myths, in reality. Most Russians, including the professor and the pensioner, are indeed far worse off today, at least economically, than they were before the collapse of communism. Prices for most goods and services have increased tenfold since January. And for the first time in their lives, millions of Russians face the threat of unemployment.

But beyond even these economic hardships is the sense that the great lie continues, that it has merely taken on a new name and a flashy new image; that the same people who brought their nation to ruin are still in power, only now they call themselves capitalists and democrats. The rules may have changed a little, but the game, and the lie, remain the same.

Perhaps nowhere is this sense of despair greater than in the bleak settlements that lie in the Amur River basin, at the furthest end of the trans-Siberian railroad—the starting point for one visitor's six-week journey across the greatest land mass on earth, a journey on a railroad once belittled by a British diplomat as "rusty streaks of iron through the vastness of nothing to the extremities of nowhere," a fitting description, many Russians believe, of the new journey they've just begun.

Observations on non-deadline writing

What makes a great non-deadline story? Is it one that reads like a novel you can't put down? Is it one that offers details so specific that you can almost see it yourself? Is it one that pulls you in so far that the end of the story leaves you wanting to read even more?

It's all those things, of course. And that's what the very best stories in the non-deadline category did. The writers made their stories so compelling that readers were pulled effortlessly along.

The winner in the category, the Louisville *Courier-Journal's* Michael Jennings, did a magnificent job of telling a personal story of his search for the father who had abandoned him and his mother years earlier. The story, run as a series of chapters rather than as one long piece, read like a serial. The twists and turns left readers wondering how it all would end, but they were unable to skip to the last page to find out. Instead, they had to wait for the next day's paper.

His description of characters may have been the strongest part of his series. Deftly weaving the different personalities into the stories gave the total package a unifying thread.

The two runners-up in this category offered similar treats for the readers.

The Providence Journal's Randall Richards submitted a series that read like a Russian novel. His story about an American man who met, fell in love with, and married a Siberian woman told the story of Siberian life through American eyes. It left readers wanting to know more about this man and his family who fought the bureaucracy to build a dream home before he died of cancer.

The Baltimore Sun's Richard O'Mara produced similarly moving pieces in his dispatches from Somalia. Readers learned first-hand the results of famine and political chaos. O'Mara translated the tragedy in Somalia into a moving story for Baltimore readers.

What characterized all the best non-deadline pieces was one thing: The writing itself made the stories fascinating reads. It's hard for readers to ask for more than that.

Jane Healy, Editor
The Orlando Sentinel

Sam Stanton

Deadline Writing

SAM STANTON, 33, a senior writer at *The Sacramento Bee,* witnessed the first execution in California in 25 years, and put the readers there beside him.

Stanton was born in Lincoln, Nebraska. He is married to his metro editor, Marjie Lundstrom. Stanton left the University of Arizona in Tucson in 1982, one semester short of a degree in journalism. Instead, he worked for *The Arizona Republic* from 1982 to 1991, and then joined *The Sacramento Bee.*

Sam Stanton and 17 other journalists witnessed the death of Robert Alton Harris. Stanton decided to take his readers to the scene by writing what he saw and heard, but not about his own emotions. His disciplined prose, his good eye and ear, and the transparency of his style spare the reader nothing.

Congratulations, Sam.

After life full of violence, Harris goes peacefully

APRIL 22, 1992

SAN QUENTIN—In the end, Robert Alton Harris seemed determined to go peacefully, a trait that had eluded him in the 39 violent and abusive years he spent on Earth.

As the cyanide fumes rose up to his face in the San Quentin gas chamber, he inhaled deeply and stared straight ahead, barely moving until death throes convulsed his body.

His trademark smirk was gone, replaced by a haunting look of sadness spawned by one last hellish night of fighting for his life and two predawn journeys to the gas chamber.

Harris, the murderer of two 16-year-old boys, made his first trip at 3:49 a.m., when he was strapped in a chair for 12 minutes. But with barely a minute to spare before the cyanide pellets were to be dropped, a surprise court order was called in, delaying the execution.

Within two hours he was walked back to the chamber and hurriedly subjected to cyanide gas poisoning that killed him at 6:21 a.m.

His final night was spent in a small metal cell with only a bare mattress, a minister and a constant stream of updates on the legal battles that appeared to have drained him by dawn.

When he entered the chamber for the second and final time at 6:01 a.m., Harris looked meekly at the four dozen witnesses and appeared to accept that after so long, he was going to die for the 1978 murders of Michael Baker and John Mayeski.

He went almost peacefully, mouthing the message to one guard watching, "It's all right."

He then craned his neck backward and to the side until he caught the eye of San Diego Police Detective Steve Baker, whose son he had murdered.

"I'm sorry," Harris mouthed.

Behind the thick windows, Baker nodded back but remained expressionless. The time for remorse had passed, he said.

"When you're sitting in the gas chamber, saying you're sorry is a little bit too little and a little bit too late," he would say later.

Within a minute of Harris' silent apology, the gas had begun to rise about him, and he sucked it deeply into his lungs.

Within minutes, he gasped, moaned and drooled until his head eased forward into his chest and he died.

Before entering the chamber, Harris borrowed a line from a recent popular movie (*Bill and Ted's Bogus Journey*). "You can be a king or a street sweeper, but everybody dances with the grim reaper," San Quentin Warden Daniel Vasquez reported him saying.

Yet the bravado appeared to be false.

While other gas chamber victims have thrashed and fought the gas, Harris appeared to give himself up to it.

He never clenched the arms of the chair to which he was strapped, and his muscular body moved in a slow, almost graceful response to the asphyxiation.

He didn't move after 6:08 a.m. but was not pronounced dead until about 13 minutes later, an event that brought an almost rapture-like smile of joy to the face of Sharron Mankins, Michael Baker's mother.

Harris' lawyers had finally failed in their attempts to spare him from the lethal gas on the grounds that it is cruel and unusual punishment.

But the events preceding his death were on a fine line between delayed justice and mental torture.

Scheduled to die at 12:01 a.m. Tuesday, Harris had begun Monday resigned to his fate, officials said.

He bid farewell to some of the guards he had become close to in his 13 years on death row, then moved to a visiting area at 8:30 a.m. to meet with family and friends.

By 6:22 p.m., he had been taken to the condemned prisoner's cell steps from the chamber, where he was to eat his last meal and spend the last 5½ hours of his life.

Instead, he spent nearly 12 hours there as a federal appeals court in San Francisco and the U.S. Supreme Court fought pitched legal battles over whether he would die.

Stay after stay after stay was handed down by the federal court seeking delays, but attorneys for the state of California pounced on each with appeals that overturned them.

Up until 11 p.m., California Department of Corrections officials were prepared to proceed on schedule with what they call the "execution ritual."

But the legal battles pushed it back, first past 1 a.m., then 2 a.m., and finally 3.

Outside the prison gates, the anti-death penalty forces had dwindled to a handful, while inside, few noises were heard save the roar of the generators from the television trucks gathered to cover the event.

But at 3:06 a.m., the word came down swiftly. All 18 media witnesses to the execution were to proceed to two waiting shuttle buses outside. Immediately.

They piled in after emptying their pockets of everything—wallets, pens, pencils, notebooks—except one piece of photo identification.

The shuttles roared off up the hill into the center of the huge prison complex, one racing so quickly toward the death house that its open door slammed into a security gate that was not opened fast enough.

The second followed closely behind, abandoning one witness who was forced to run to the assembly point—a snack bar by the gas chamber building.

"We're minutes away from execution," shouted Tipton Kindel, the Corrections Department spokesman.

After searches of all 18, the witnesses were marched out into the moonlit, cloudless night. They moved across a street under the watch of a sharpshooter and several guards, creating ominous echoing bangs as each stepped on a loose manhole cover.

Inside the witness room, friends and relatives of Mayeski and Baker already stood toward the back of the room on two rising platforms. Closer to the death chamber, standing before a railing several feet away from the windows, were more witnesses and relatives.

Away toward a far corner was a cluster of guests Harris had invited, including his older brother, Randall.

At 3:49 a.m., three guards firmly gripping Harris walked him into the chamber and held him while he was strapped into Chair B, one of two inside the apple-green contraption.

He appeared to have tears in his eyes momentarily, but within a minute gave a thumbs-up sign and wink to the onlookers.

He was dressed in a new, short-sleeved work shirt and denim trousers, his brownish yet graying hair pulled back in a slight ponytail.

In the background, a faint ringing could be heard behind the chamber door.

"Oh, God," gasped one of the women from the Baker and Mayeski contingent.

It sounded momentarily like a telephone ring, and witnesses nervously eyed each other as they considered whether last-minute reprieves came only in movies.

After a minute, the concern appeared groundless. Harris was left in the chamber and the minutes began to tick away as everyone awaited the gas.

At 3:53 a.m. he mouthed to a guard, "I can't move."

He looked around. Back to his friends and relatives. Over to four guards standing toward the corner of the witness room. Up at the reporters craning and contorting to see him over the shoulders of those at the railing.

He flexed his hands and shook his head as though agitated, wanting to get it over with. He appeared to shrug toward the reporters.

A few more minutes passed.

Suddenly, a subterranean groaning began to rumble through the room, the sound that might be caused by the release of hydrochloric acid into the holding tank under his seat, with the cyanide packets suspended above.

It was now 3:58 a.m., and even Harris thought it was time. "Let's pull the lever," he appeared to say, then laughed.

But another minute passed as he looked about impatiently, and some heard a voice from behind the chamber say, "Turn the water off."

Still nothing happened, and at 4 a.m. Harris closed his eyes and bowed his head, then looked up again.

Within a minute the chamber door was pulled open suddenly. Burly, purposeful guards expertly unstrapped and hustled him out of the chamber as he looked up in confusion.

"Ladies and gentleman," prison spokesman Vernell Crittendon began to say.

But it was obvious. There was another stay of execution.

The witnesses were escorted out, and they learned that Harris had been within minutes of death when a judge telephoned the prison to delay the execution. The groaning sound they heard was the acid being withdrawn from the reservoir as officials rushed to put the brakes on the ritual.

Outside, officers escorting the media witnesses assumed wrongly that the execution had been carried out.

"Devastating, huh?" one said after seeing the shocked looks on the faces of those emerging.

It was—but to the Baker and Mayeski relatives, not to the Harris guests.

Marilyn Clark, a sister of Mayeski who had tears in her eyes through much of the ordeal, looked stunned.

Linda Herring, Michael Baker's sister, grabbed her head in disbelief. California Attorney General Dan Lungren's face fell with disappointment.

Across the room, Harris' friends and relatives stood in shocked silence, holding their hands and their breath at the thought that he might be saved once again.

All the witnesses were returned to their waiting areas away from reporters while prison officials announced the state's intent to overturn the stay.

By 5:45 a.m., Harris had lost his final legal fight. Once again, the reporters were rushed onto the buses. They roared off again, this time stranding two witnesses who had to hitch a ride in a car.

The searches this time were quick, and the officers hurried the witnesses into the chamber.

The other witnesses already were present, and at 6:01 a.m. a pumping sound could be heard. This time, it was clear the acid was flowing inward to the tank under the chair.

In the same minute, Harris was brought in once again, and three guards strapped him in.

This time, there was a noticeable difference. He appeared almost as lifeless as he would be in a matter of minutes.

His face was etched with lines, and his eyes were large and sad looking. He barely appeared to move on his own, apparently drained by the sleepless night and the emotional toll of the event two hours before.

He shut his eyes, then opened them and mouthed "It's all right" to a guard and "I'm sorry" to Baker.

By 6:05 a.m. it became clear that Harris would die. No one heard the pellets plunk into the holding tanks of acid, nor saw the gas rise up.

But he suddenly began breathing in and out very forcefully. His eyes rolled into the back of his head, which leaned slowly forward and then all the way back.

A few minutes later it moved forward again. At times, his mouth was half-open. At others, his eyes were slits.

He convulsed involuntarily, and moaned, then gasped and convulsed again. He took deep breaths of the poison air as his head moved slowly forward again, then shook with yet another convulsion.

At 6:07 a.m., Harris appeared to finally be at rest. His head was bowed forward on his chest, and his eyes were closed.

But a minute later his body struggled for survival as his head moved upward with a gasp, then down with another.

He began to drool, and his body once again was wracked with convulsions.

By 6:12 a.m., his body gave up the fight and Harris slowly died.

"The boy's dead," whispered one witness from near the Mayeski and Baker relatives.

Sharron Mankins grinned. She had carried the pain for so long of the description of the boys' deaths.

She knew the story well: how Harris riddled the boys' bodies with bullets after stealing their car for a bank robbery; how he had chased one down and told him before he killed him, "God can't help you now, boy. You're going to die."

She had heard the claims that Harris was not responsible, that he had been abused from before premature birth when his father kicked his mother in the womb, that he had been subjected to fetal alcohol poisoning, that he had been repeatedly abused as a child.

But she and the others had maintained that their pain could be eased only by the finality his death would bring.

Marilyn Clark looked upward.

Linda Herring stood pensively, her arms folded across her chest.

But the minutes dragged on.

By 6:16 a.m., Crittendon glanced nervously at his watch.

In the next minute, relatives of Harris' victims began to whisper among themselves.

Before that, most in the chamber had been silent, except for the reporters who whispered descriptions and times to each other.

At 6:20 a.m., clanking sounds could be heard faintly in the rooms behind the chamber, and two minutes later there was a knock on the steel-riveted door that led from it to the witness room. It opened slightly, and a piece of paper was thrust out.

A guard read the wordy announcement that contained a simple message:

Robert Alton Harris had been declared legally dead at 6:21 a.m.

The witnesses filed outside, into the bright sunlight.

After 25 years and nine days, California's gas chamber was back in operation.

Bee staff writer Sam Stanton was among 18 reporters who witnessed the execution of Robert Alton Harris.

Observations and questions

1) The headline, "After life full of violence, Harris goes peacefully," uses three words from Stanton's lead: "In the end, Robert Alton Harris seemed determined to *go peacefully,* a trait that had eluded him in the 39 *violent* and abusive years he spent on Earth." Think about the effect on the readers of this duplication. Does it enhance or detract? Try to compose your own headline for this complex story.

2) Stanton deliberately chose not to write in the first person despite his presence at the event. Imagine this story rewritten by Stanton entirely in first-person narration. What would you gain, and what would you lose?

3) This long piece uses cinematic cutting back and forth across scenes and characters and time. Think about this technique in terms of enriching the readers' experience of the event against the risk of confusing them.

4) Redesign this story so that the events unfold in strictly chronological order. Would the story become more or less confusing? Would you lose some chances for juxtaposing key elements?

5) Stanton uses 12 named characters and a number of unnamed ones in this story. Notice how he spreads them out, keeps them sorted into groups, and reminds us who they are as time passes. What would he gain by naming more of the characters, such as the minister and the various guards, and what would he lose?

6) Notice how Stanton uses explicit time markers throughout to keep the readers oriented. Why don't these time phrases become tedious? How does Stanton keep the readers from noticing them?
   Now ask the same questions about space markers.

7) Few news stories contain any sound at all. Examine each sound in this story and speculate on its effect on the reader. Why do we use this device so little?

8) In the middle, Stanton says: "It sounded momentarily like a telephone ring, and witnesses nervously eyed

each other as they considered whether last-minute reprieves came only in movies." Normally we don't indulge in such mind-reading. How can we indicate how
and what people think without cluttering up the story
with lots of attribution apparatus?

9) Stanton effectively uses faces throughout this story.
Look at each instance and study what effect Stanton creates. Notice how he uses speech to frame gestures and
vice-versa.

10) Because of its structure, the story repeats wording,
some quotes, and scenes. Examine in detail how Stanton
uses repetition with variation to deepen the readers'
sense of events.

11) At the end, as Harris died, the author swerves off
into a digression on Sharron Mankins. Study the con-
tents of this passage and imagine where else you could
put it whole or some of its parts. What purpose does it
serve where it is?

12) Stanton closes: "After 25 years and nine days, California's gas chamber was back in operation." Debate
the merits and demerits of this sentence as an ending.
What other sentences or passages in the story would
make good kickers?

A conversation with
Sam Stanton

DON FRY: "Senior Writer" sounds rather grand. What does your title mean at *The Sacramento Bee*?

SAM STANTON: Well, it means you work your own hours. It doesn't mean a lot in terms of the assignments you get. That really depends on the individual reporter.

Is there more than one senior writer?

Yeah. There are quite a few here.

Do you originate stories as well as take assignments?

I do both. I went to Somalia twice last year, and they let me do that because I asked way back in June before it was a big story. But there are also stories assigned that I just knock out. I return from Somalia one day, and the next day I'm doing a weather story. This can really be a humbling business, no matter how inflated your ego gets.

Keeps your fancy title in perspective. Did you ask for the execution story?

Yeah. I knew the execution was coming up, so I told the editors I'd be willing to do it, because I thought I could do a good job.

Why did you want it?

It's the kind of story that doesn't come along but once every couple of decades. This was

---

[Editor's Note: I have heavily edited and rearranged this conversation for brevity and clarity, and recomposed the questions.]

going to be the first execution in this state in 25
or 26 years. I constantly try to challenge myself
to do better stories and more interesting stories. Basically I'm almost obsessed with doing
stories that other people don't want to do, or
getting into very competitive stories. This was a
very competitive story.

You bet.

The biggest papers in California were there,
from the *L.A. Times* on down, and I wanted to
prove to myself that I could hold my own with
them. I got no arguments because there weren't
a lot of people lining up to say, "I'd like to go
stand in a gas chamber and watch someone
die." [Laughter]

The paper regarded it as a plum assignment?

Yeah. Well, I think so. But Harris had been in
the gas chamber before and got pulled out,
with executions getting cancelled at the last
minute. So I wasn't convinced it was really going to happen.
   I did a series of stories about who he was,
what his crime had been, how the gas chamber
works, that type of thing. Arizona had an execution one month before Harris died, their
first execution in about 25 years. So I had the
benefit of being able to call some old friends of
mine who had been witnesses to that execution,
not only for stories I was doing, but to ask
them personally, "How was it? Did you have
any problems? What can I expect?"

Were they right?

Well, I had a mixture of responses. Some of
them had been really upset and moved by what
they saw, and others said, "Well, it was no big
deal. It didn't bother me." I called them because the one in Arizona had been pretty
graphic. In the last moments of his life, the

condemned man made an obscene gesture to the attorney general and thrashed around. I wanted to have all that in my mind. I wanted to know what I was going to be seeing in this place.

So you went in well prepared?

You have to, on a story like this. It isn't like going to a city council meeting. I wanted to know exactly what was supposed to happen, so that I wouldn't have to be tied down marveling at what I was seeing and what was going on. I tried to do as much backgrounding as I possibly could, particularly as the thing got nearer and nearer, and the pressure began building from the outside.

Were you thinking about the death penalty?

I had to do several interviews with reporters who asked me, "What's your personal view on the death penalty?" And I kept saying, "I'm not going to tell you." They would laugh and say, "Well, everybody else did." But how can they expect their readers to look at their stories objectively?

Right. So what is your opinion on the death penalty?

None of your business, Don. [Laughter] I'm not going to tell you. I'm pleased that before and after I wrote my stories, I got the same number of letters saying, "You're an anti-death-penalty loon" as I got from people saying, "You're obviously pro-death-penalty," so I assume I kept my own feelings in check.

Did you read other stories about executions?

Yeah. I had read quite a few, all the ones that came out of the Arizona execution. But one had the most impact on me. I was sitting at my desk, and a reporter who sits across from me said, "You've got to read our execution story from 1966, by a guy who worked here at *The Bee*." So I found the clips, and it was an incredible story, just incredible. He had written it on deadline, really up against the gun. That drove me to prepare myself even more, because I kept thinking, "I've got to be able to at least match this guy's story." That was a hell of a good story.

What made it good?

The details. The color. It wasn't too..., I don't know if "flashy" is the word..., it wasn't too graphic. He wasn't trying to overwrite. He wasn't swinging for the fences. He was just telling the people what he saw.

Would you call it *restrained*?

Yeah. And it was *not* in the first person.

At the execution, what kind of notes could you take?

Basically the only notes I took were something like "drool" or "cough." That really is all that you could do in that physical setup.

Almost at the end of the story, you say, "Before that, most in the chamber had been silent, except for the reporters who whispered descriptions and times to each other." The reporters fed each other information?

Yeah. We were standing in two rows on risers in a half circle around the chamber itself. We were stuffed off into one corner, with the family members of the victims and the family members of Harris on the other sides. The chamber has small, square windows. Witnesses lined up directly in front of the chamber, so we were looking through people's shoulders and heads.

We all had a different view of Harris while he was seated in the chamber, so we were all saying, "Okay, he's doing this." The reporters on the other end, who couldn't see it, would scribble that. And later, we doubled-checked times.

You agreed ahead of time to pool information.

Well, it was understood we were in a pool situation. But I don't remember sitting down beforehand and making any kind of agreement like that. It was pretty obvious that, unless we all cooperated, none of us would get the complete story.

What happens to your competitive urges in that case?

I figured the competition would happen in the writing. We had all signed agreements that when we came out of the chamber, we would sit for interviews afterwards. Out of a sense of fairness, I don't think that if I had seen something, I could have kept it to myself. And I was hoping that other reporters weren't doing that to me.

Did they? [Laughter]

I don't think so.

So this is pure competition, purely on writing, not access.

Yeah.

Did you have a sense of camaraderie with the other people in the room?

No. Not at all. I had a sense that I had to come out of there with the best story.

Harris was declared dead at 6:21 a.m. How far away was your deadline?

We're a morning paper, so I had until five or six. I was sweating it, because I had arrived at San Quentin at two in the afternoon the previous day. I hadn't been sleeping well before then, and we'd been up all night long. I had to drive back a couple of hours to the *Bee* newsroom to file the story, and I was just dog-tired. I knew that I had to get that story written as quickly as I could before I started to lose some impressions of what I had seen.

Did you work on the story on the way back?

I was driving and trying to come up with a lead for about five miles. That's how I do a lot of my stories when I'm on the road: the perfect lead and story just kind of appear on the windshield. But this time, it wasn't coming because I didn't know what else was in the package, what the other reporters from my paper were writing. So I just stopped thinking about it, turned on the radio, and listened to music, and occasionally I would think of a word I wanted to use. I thought of the word "graceful." I remembered the manhole cover.

I just kept my mind on a couple of things like that, and I drove. I went home and showered and changed clothes, and came in to the paper. They put me into an unoccupied office in the back, and I locked the door and didn't take any phone calls or talk to anybody; I just sat there and wrote the thing.

Do you organize stories by thinking up leads?

Once I come up with the lead, it tends to flow from there. I'm not the type who can write the body of the story, and then come back and do the lead. I've got to have the lead first, or at least a fake lead. Then I go on, and later, I come back and tinker with the lead.

I'm the opposite. I always write the lead last,

and never tinker with it. So how did you put this story together?

This one was tougher than most. I wanted to get the reader into the gas chamber as quickly as possible, but I also wanted the readers to know up front that this guy was dragged in there twice. I wanted it to be obvious to the reader that I had seen it, and that they were going to see what had happened in there. I wanted to do that without the first person.

So they're in the chamber. But how do I get back out of the chamber and into the background of the story? It wasn't that difficult, as it turned out, but I wasn't quite sure how I was going to do it.

Right. Do you write the parts and move them around?

No. I usually bang out the whole thing, then occasionally go back and change some things. On this one, I went back to the lead. I'd been writing in the office in the back, and I didn't know what the other reporters were doing, so I had a more general lead on it, about Harris finally being executed after all these years. One of my editors tiptoed back there and said, "Look, I don't want to interfere with your story, but we kind of peeked at it, and we just want you to know that we've already covered the court angle in a separate story." I said, "Fine. Go away." [Laughter] So I changed the lead.

They "peeked at it" electronically?

Yeah. In our system, the editors can look at what you're writing. I suppose none of them wanted to come back and talk to me, because they weren't quite sure of my frame of mind. I think they were peeking because, when I sat down, I said, "I'm going to try something different here." I think they were afraid I was going to do it in the first person.

When did you decide against first person?

I never intended doing that. When I told them I was going to do something different, I meant I'm *not* doing it in the first person. I had seen a lot of those.

Ahh, newsroom communications! What's wrong with first person?

Well, I just don't think I'm that important. I'm paid to tell people what I've seen, but I'm not sure the readers care how *I* feel about it. I saw the same thing happen in Somalia, a lot of first-person stories coming out of there. I'm not sure my thoughts are more important than some kid starving to death or getting shot, or this man being put to death by the state.

I would have had to give my opinion, which would have colored the story either way. It just seemed intrusive. My job was to go in there and tell people exactly what happened. Let them make up their own minds about whether this is good or bad. I tried to tell them what I saw.

How did you want readers to react?

I wanted them to know that this is a really emotional thing for a lot of people. It's very tense in there. It's very eerie. But I didn't want them to say, "Gee, executions are bad," or "Gee, I'm glad we finally killed him." It's not up to me to make that happen.

So you had no political agenda here?

Not at all. If any of the reporters did, they shouldn't have been covering this thing. That's not what we're in this business for.

So you banged it out. Did you revise much?

What you see is pretty much what I wrote the first time through. I went back and changed a few descriptions. But I really agonized over one paragraph.

Which paragraph?

Here it is: "But the events preceding his death were on a fine line between delayed justice and mental torture." I was really concerned, because I didn't want people to say, "Aha, this is how he feels about the death penalty." I wanted to explain that this man had been taken in there twice. I wanted them to think about that. You're sitting there, and all of a sudden, it's like in a movie: the door opens up, the phone rings, they're dragging you out of the chamber, and they're saying, "You're not going to die after all." And then an hour or two later, they say, "I'm sorry. Time to go back!"

Just an awful scene, really tough to write....

Yeah. I wanted it to be fair. I didn't want it to be commentary. I wanted it to be reporting. But I think it turned out well.

I do too. Was this piece edited much?

Not much at all. We were trying to make it a certain length. I was determined to do it to exactly the right length, because I knew I'd be at home when the cutting began, and I didn't want any cutting. I wasn't sure I was going to have the strength to come back into the newsroom.

Did you agree on length before you wrote?

No. I never do. An editor came in and said, "Well, what are you looking at: 40, 45 inches?" I said, "No, I've got to have 80, 85." We negotiated throughout the day. When I finished it, I said, "Look, it *is* much longer than what you wanted, but I want you to read it first, and then tell me about space." They came back and said, "You're right, we're going to leave it alone. We'll fit everything in."

Were they measuring it over your shoulder electronically?

Sure they were. For all they knew, I was sitting there in the corner, drooling in emotional upheaval. [Laughter]

Somehow we keep coming back to drool. Well, here's your lead: "In the end, Robert Alton Harris seemed determined to go peacefully, a trait that had eluded him in the 39 violent and abusive years he had spent on earth.
    "As the cyanide fumes rose up to his face in the San Quentin gas chamber, he inhaled deeply and stared straight ahead, barely moving until death throes convulsed his body.
    "His trademark smirk was gone, replaced by a haunting look of sadness spawned by one last hellish night of fighting for his life and two predawn journeys to the gas chamber."
    You said you were playing with the lead and the word "graceful" in the car, but you didn't use "graceful" in the lead.

No. But it's further down in the story. I didn't want to say in the lead that this man died gracefully, because that's not how I saw it. "Graceful" refers to his struggle with the gas. He wasn't jerking, and he wasn't frantic. He was almost in slow motion, as his body was convulsing. That seemed graceful to me. I think "peacefully" was the most important part, because he really was subdued, and that's not the personality that got him there.

You focus on his face. Was that a conscious decision?

Yeah. I thought people would want to know what he looked like, whether he was weeping or cursing. There really isn't that much else to focus on anyway, because he was strapped down so tightly in that chair. You can't see the fumes, so you're looking at this man's face, or at the witnesses. You had that choice.

Right. The headline, "After Life Full of Violence, Harris Goes Peacefully," steals your lead.

Oh, that didn't bother me. I think it's a good headline. It's accurate, and people were going to read this story.

How did the editors react after you turned the piece in?

They really liked it. They said, "Great. We love it. Now get out of here." [Laughter] I finished it before three in the afternoon. I took a short break to go get something to eat and let it sit in the computer before I turned it in. I did a radio interview or two, and I talked to some friends. Then I shot it over to their baskets.

How long did it sit?

Oh, not more than an hour. I just wanted to be sure that some lightning bolt wasn't going to hit that I needed to get in.

Did any hit?

No. But I had those radio interviews to do, and I thought that maybe that would jog something in my mind that I needed to add.

We call that "letting it cool off." It's easier to see it when you come back to it. You can get lost in the words. How did you keep the time sequences straight, and how did you help the reader keep them straight?

Well, I tried to key in only on the really important times: the time of death, which the prison officials announced; the time he entered the chamber; the time they dropped the cyanide pill; that type of thing. There aren't that many times in here. It may seem like it though, because there were two visits to the chamber, and both times, we were checking off the times.

The last part is chronological.

Yeah. The last part was the easiest to write: At 6:05, he smells the gas. Two minutes later, his head is down. This is the difficult part: explaining how he dealt with the gas, the drooling, and the convulsions, and some things.

What made this part difficult?

Well, it wasn't pleasant to watch. I didn't want to seem voyeuristic. I was trying to think about the drool and the body racked with convulsions. I didn't want it to be too graphic for some people, but I wanted them to know exactly what happened.

The reporters were trying to do their jobs, but it was not a peaceful ceremony. There were reporters shouting out, "Look, he's drooling. He's drooling. Did you get the drool?" Things like that. At one point, one of the reporters asked one of the witnesses to move over so she could get a better view of him dying. There were family members of the victims, who were obviously very happy about what was going on. I got some of that in the story.

Was Harris's family also in that same room?

Yeah. They were across the room from us, and, as you can imagine, their eyes were filled with hatred.

So both families were in the same room with the reporters?

Right.

Oh boy, how tense! Had you ever seen anyone die before?

No. I'd seen traffic accidents and things, but I'd never seen anything like this. Afterward, I saw a lot of death in Somalia, but it's not the same thing. You see somebody die from a bullet wound, or you see somebody die from starvation. But this was the concerted effort by the state of California to put someone to death. It's an eerie experience, I've got to tell you.

A TV reporter would now ask you how you felt, but I'm not going to ask you that. I want to know how you dealt with your emotions.

I kept telling myself that it was just a story, and I think a lot of the reporters felt the same way I did. In the end, while we were shouting out times and descriptions to each other, it was almost like covering a press conference.

I think it was easier than we feared, because we'd been in there twice. The first time took the edge off. The first time, as they were walking us in, I wasn't sure I was going to make it without getting sick to my stomach. I was convinced the guy behind me was going to get very sick. Everybody was very nervous. The second time, it was clear it was going to happen. We were just so tired, and by then had been subjected to it once.

Did anybody get sick?

No. Another witness later got drunk. That was a feeling I could understand. I knew I was going home to do the same thing. But it never really struck me. I don't want to say that it never really bothered me, because I did dream about it. I had a couple of dreams before I saw it, and a couple after I saw it, but it was nothing like a nightmare, where you wake up in a cold sweat. It never really hung with me the way these things have with some other reporters. I know some who had emotional upheavals about seeing this type of thing.

But it was a story to cover, and it was important that we be there, and that's the way I looked at it.

I'm wondering what makes you different. All the reporters would probably say the same thing, but many were deeply affected in ways that you weren't.

I don't mean to sound cold-hearted, but my job was to get the story and bring it back, and that's what I tried to do.

Okay. Let's talk about quoting, a lot of quotations under hard conditions. How do you take down quotations?

Most of my notes are quotes I plan to use, figures I need to write down. But I'm not one of those reporters who fills up a notebook. Generally, I take down longer quotes than these. I rarely use a tape recorder, almost never.

Do you write down the *whole* quotation?

Yeah. I do it in a strange shorthand I've developed. I'll skip a word or two, but I try to get the main thing down, because it's important to quote the person accurately. You don't want to be making up the quote later on.

But you didn't have much paper to take notes on....

Yeah. Right. Just loose legal-size pieces of paper. The only time I had trouble was inside the chamber at the end, when the guard came down and read the death notice. It was this wordy, bureaucratic legalese that basically said, "He's dead." That's the way I wrote it at the very end of the story. I called it a "wordy announcement."

You didn't quote it.

I didn't have the quote. I know I could have got the piece of paper, but it didn't mean anything. What he was trying to say, in a less than straightforward fashion, was, "Well, we did it; he's dead."

This piece is very lightly attributed.

Well, that's because I saw most of what is in here, and attribution slows you down a lot of the time.

Does *The Bee* attribute heavily?

No. I've worked for editors who demand attribution in almost every paragraph, and I don't agree with that. If it's obvious that what you're writing is true, you don't want to bog your writing down with attribution. If they didn't trust me, I had no business working for them.

Well, I know some nervous editors who would attribute every paragraph, even with you there.

Yeah. But if that had happened, we wouldn't be talking, would we? [Laughter]

No, we would not. Listen to this description: "He was dressed in a new, short-sleeved work shirt and denim trousers, his brownish yet graying hair pulled back in a slight ponytail." We don't describe much in newspapers. How did you decide what to describe?

I tried to tell people the story so they could picture it in their minds, almost like watching it on television. Everybody in this state knows what Harris's face looks like, because he had been on television for so many years here. But they didn't know what he was going to be looking like *there*. He's got this work shirt. He has jeans on. His hair is graying, and it's in a ponytail. It's pretty simple.

You don't tell us what color his shirt is.

I'm not sure I could tell in that light. The light was really strange, almost like being inside an aquarium. There was a greenish glow, and I couldn't tell.

Listen to another piece of description: "His face was etched with lines, and his eyes were large and sad looking. He barely appeared to move on his own, apparently drained by the sleepless night and the emotional toll of the event two hours before." Very restrained. You represent emotion there by outward signs.

That was the way I saw it. His eyes *were* sad looking. He clearly was sad, but I didn't say that. I said he was *sad looking*. You don't need to pound it into the reader's head. You give them the chance to conjure up their own images. You can really overwrite on something like this, and I didn't want to do that.

In newswriting, unlike novels, we can't read minds, so we tend to describe things from the outside. Listen to this: "It sounded momentarily like a telephone ring, and witnesses nervously eyed each other as they considered whether last-minute reprieves came only in movies." Well, maybe a little bit of mind reading? [Laughter]

Well, it would have been, except that some of the witnesses said afterwards that's what they talked about. Some of the other witnesses clearly were nervous. In the previous paragraph, a woman was obviously horrified at the thought that that telephone meant Harris wasn't going to be put to death. You could tell.

Anybody who's been a reporter for a long time, who has watched people under different strains and pressures, can tell when somebody is nervous. And it was pretty clear that people were nervous about what that ring meant. I wasn't even sure it was a telephone. That's why I said, "It *sounded* like a telephone ring."

Very carefully phrased.

As it turns out, it was a phone, but I wasn't certain.

The real temptation in something like this is to read the *killer's* mind. In fact, a lot of the classic accounts of executions look into the mind of the killer.

Yeah, but it was hard this time, because he wasn't giving interviews, not in several years. All of us had talked to his attorneys about how he was doing, and to his friends about how he felt, but nobody had talked to *him*. That was a hard thing to tell. It was clear that he was sad and almost uncomfortable with the attention. But there is just so much you can tell by looking at somebody through a big, thick glass window.

I think you told a lot, and I think you admired him a little.

I don't know that I admired *him*. I think I admired the way he went.

We're back to your word "graceful," aren't we?

Yeah. I was taken by the fact that he did turn to Baker and say, "I'm sorry." He didn't fight the gas. I don't know if "admiration" is the right word.

What's the right word?

I don't know. Maybe you're right. He didn't go thrashing and snarling. But you have to feel sorry for anybody who's being executed, as you're watching his execution, particularly anybody who had gone through being strapped down twice. Boy, that had to be the most difficult thing you can imagine. I guess I admired the way he handled that. He was clearly beaten down and exhausted. He had to strain to say "I'm sorry" to Baker. He had to really go against his restraints, but he wanted to get that message out. He looked over at us at one point and shrugged.

Ohhhh, he could *see you*?

Yeah. He looked me right in the eye. He kind of shrugged. I thought: "My God, how calm could you possibly be at this moment?"

That's called admiration.

Yeah. I suppose.

You see, it's easy to write an execution story if you just paint the monster, but when you empathize with him, that's different.

Maybe he had been in his life, but I didn't see a monster sitting there.

Journalists read this series for advice on how to do things, so I want you to give me a bulleted list of suggestions about covering something this difficult.

It's simple. *You've got to be prepared.* That's the most basic thing in covering any kind of story. But in something this important, you've got to call people who have been through it. You've got to read as much as you can about it. You've got to familiarize yourself with what is supposed to happen and what has happened in the past. I called people all over the country who had witnessed an execution, and I talked to people who had been outside prisons during these things. I read as much as I possibly could. I called some government officials who had witnessed the execution in Arizona to get a non-media perspective.

You've got to get as much information as you can. If you're going to be writing on deadline and you're going to be tired, you don't have time to go back to the clips. You don't have time to make a call to get that one fact that you were meaning to get but didn't. You've got to have as much of this stuff out of the way as you can, so you can concentrate on what you're seeing.

Bullet one: BE PREPARED.

I sound like a Boy Scout. [Laughter]

Better a Boy Scout than *un*prepared. Then what?

You've got to be ready to dodge left and right. It's not going to go the way you think all the time, as this one obviously didn't. I had to be flexible. I had a computer with me because I was pretty sure that the execution wasn't going to take place, and I was going to be filing some story about another reprieve or another delay. And, in fact, I did file several stories that night, adding on and on as the delays came.

Bullet two: BE FLEXIBLE.

The next thing is detail. Get that color down even if you don't use it. You don't know if you're going to need it or not. I learned a lot from this experience that I used later in Somalia. When I got to Somalia, I was taking notes the way I always do. But then at night, I would stay up late, or I would get up very early, and I would write a journal of every single thing I had seen in a separate notebook. That way, first, I could have my notes safe with two sets of them, and second, I could pull out any color that maybe I hadn't scribbled down in the notes. Even on a deadline story, scribble down as much color as you can. Maybe I should have been able to get the color of his shirt....

Bullet three: LOTS OF DETAIL (and get the color of the shirt). Any advice for afterwards?

Afterwards, don't dwell on it. Go on to your next story.

From everything I've heard you say, I think remembering that you're a journalist helped you deal with this situation. Just saying, "I have a job to do. This is what I do."

You're right. This is not something you're *experiencing*. This is a story you're *covering*. You have to keep saying to yourself, "Nobody cares how I feel about this. I'm writing a story."

Bullet four, last but foremost: REMEMBER WHO YOU ARE, AND JUST DO IT. Now that you've won this prize, is there a dream assignment you'd like?

You know, I hate to call covering an execution a dream assignment, but that's one of the things on the mental list of stories I've always wanted to cover, and Somalia was another. I've had some really great assignments that other reporters will never have the experience of covering, some wonderful things. Now I'm looking for a story that's new, that people haven't spotted yet. But I don't know what it is.

If you write it, it will come.

The Miami Herald

Martin Merzer

Finalist, Deadline Writing

Martin Merzer, a senior writer on the *Herald*'s enterprise team, has a B.A. in English from Hunter College of the City University of New York. He moved to Miami after six years with the Associated Press. He covered business for both organizations, and served as the *Herald*'s Jerusalem bureau chief.

Merzer's obituary tribute to Red Barber conjures up a time "when baseball broadcasters textured the game and magnified it and rendered it unforgettable." He creates a word picture of our best picturer in words.

Voice of baseball silenced at age 84

OCTOBER 23, 1992

If baseball could speak, it would have sounded like Red Barber.

Barber, whose melodious Southern voice evoked memories of peanut shells and cigar smoke and long drives to deep center field, died Thursday in Tallahassee. He was 84.

The legendary sports announcer who called himself "The Ol' Redhead" long before he was old and long after his hair faded, had suffered for weeks with an intestinal blockage, pneumonia and other ailments.

One of America's most honored and distinguished broadcasters, a man who literally talked his way into baseball's Hall of Fame, Barber described—no, embroidered—baseball games through 33 springs, summers and falls.

"He made everyone's living room a seat behind home plate," said U.S. Sen. Connie Mack, grandson of the famed baseball manager of the same name.

Barber worked for the Cincinnati Reds from 1934 to 1938, but then moved to New York, a tough-talking town where the young man with those soft Southern tones and folksy rhythms earned his greatest renown.

From 1939 to 1953, he related the melancholy exploits of the Brooklyn Dodgers, a team called "Dem Bums" by its long-suffering but ever hopeful fans.

After a salary dispute, Barber moved uptown to the Bronx, working for the more regal New York Yankees from 1954 until he was fired in 1966 for being a bit too honest about a "crowd" of 413 fans at a late-season game.

Fifteen years later, he returned to broadcasting and captivated a new generation of sports fans and other listeners with his commentary every Friday morning on National Public Radio.

His subjects: everything from the poetry of baseball to the corrupting influence of money on sports to his ever-troublesome azaleas.

A FINE STORY-TELLER

"The biggest complaint we get about the bit is it's too short," Bob Edwards, host of NPR's *Morning Edition,* said two years ago. "Red can't really tell a long story."

No, Red Barber couldn't tell a long story. But, my, how he could spin a fine one.

When Barber broadcast a game, he did more than merely relate the obvious. He knit the broad action and the tiny details into a tapestry and then colored it with his encyclopedic knowledge of baseball and his love of it.

He habitually showed up at the ballpark two hours early. There always was so much to learn.

"For three hours during the game I was a talker," Barber once said. "For two hours before it I was a listener."

He spent the formative years of his career before a radio microphone and, like other radio pioneers, he knew that if he provided the proper nutrition, his audience's imagination would flower.

"Radio is a pleasure to work in," Barber said. "Television is like day labor."

His was a time before the endless replays of televised sports, before the constant and often empty chatter of today's "play-by-play announcers," before "color analysts" spent most of their time reciting a long list of obscure statistics.

It was a time when baseball broadcasters textured the game and magnified it and rendered it unforgettable.

BARBER'S MAGIC

Listen to the magic of Red Barber and hear a bit of baseball's almost forgotten past.

A runner tagged out at second: "The gate shut on him."

A rally: "The boys sure are tearin' up the pea patch."

A fight on the field: "A rhubarb is under way."

A team in control: "They're in the catbird seat now, folks."

A massive and timely home run: "Oh, doctor!"

And think back to the moments Red Barber witnessed and shared: Mickey Owen's dropped third strike in the 1941 World Series. The shattering of baseball's color line by Jackie Robinson. Roger Maris hitting his record-breaking 61st home run in 1961.

And appreciate the inspiration that he was. Among his proteges was Vin Scully, now with the Los Angeles Dodgers and CBS Radio, and widely considered one of the best announcers in the business today.

Said Scully of his mentor: "He was the most literate baseball sports announcer that I've ever met or ever heard of."

'I WASN'T A FAN OF ANYONE'

And one of the most objective.

"I wasn't a Dodger fan, I wasn't a Yankee fan," Barber once said. "I wasn't a fan of anyone. I described that game in the best way I knew how without partiality. I think the listeners appreciated that."

That they did. They appreciated everything about him.

Walter Lanier "Red" Barber was born Feb. 17, 1908, in Columbus, Miss. As a child, he lived in Sanford, Fla., and the state remained an important part of his life.

Barber began his broadcasting career in 1930 while studying at the University of Florida. Since 1972, he had lived in Tallahassee. And the Florida Cabinet declared his 80th birthday to be "Red Barber Day," complete with a party at the state Capitol.

But perhaps his finest honor came in 1978 when he and battery-mate Mel Allen were inducted into the Baseball Hall of Fame, the first broadcasters to be enshrined there.

Barber is survived by his wife, Lylah, and daughter, Sarah.

In lieu of flowers, the family requested contributions in Barber's memory be made to the Alzheimer's Disease and Related Disorder Association.

Red Barber, whose broadcasting career spanned seven decades, dead at 84. During the World Series of a sport so much in his debt.

Diane Pucin

Finalist, Deadline Writing

Diane Pucin has covered sports for *The Philadelphia Inquirer* since 1986. Before that, she wrote sports in Columbus (Ga.), Cincinnati, and Louisville. She's married to Dan Weber, the executive sports editor of the *Bucks County Courier.*

Sports movements are notoriously hard to describe, but Pucin captures the grace and precision of world-class athletes who fight it out moment by moment, and who just happen to be 15-year-old girls.

Two girls go for one gold

JULY 31, 1992

BARCELONA—They look like two strands of spaghetti, Tatiana Goutsou and Shannon Miller. Both are blond and pale, and they bend and curl and flutter as if they have no bones.

And yet these two 15-year-olds, who could be mistaken for twins when they stand in profile, had nothing but backbone last night.

Outshining more famous teammates, Goutsou, from Ukraine, took the Olympic women's all-around gold medal by .012 points over Shannon Miller of Oklahoma. Lavinia Milosovici of Romania won the bronze medal.

The gold medal came down to the final event, which happened to be the vault for both Goutsou and Miller. They had been placed in the same rotation, competing with seven other girls on the same apparatus all evening.

Goutsou had taken the lead quickly on their first event, the high bar. She had scored a 9.95 and Miller a 9.925. Miller's coach, Steve Nunno, complained about that later, saying that Miller had bad luck in being drawn to perform first.

"She was underscored," Nunno said. "Shannon is the gold-medal winner in my eyes. She was the best."

Goutsou's lead never got any bigger, but when Miller got ready to do her two vaults, she knew she needed to be almost perfect for a chance at the gold. She was.

Miller's takeoff was perfect. Her twisting backflip off the vault was sharp. Her landing stuck flat into the mat. Nunno bounded into the air as if he were on a trampoline.

"A [perfect] 10," Nunno said. "That vault was a perfect 10."

Not according to the judges. It was scored a 9.975.

Gymnasts get two vaults and keep the higher score. Miller's second vault was not quite as solid, earning her a 9.95.

Goutsou still had her two vaults. She needed a 9.938 to tie Miller and a 9.939 to win outright. Miller was standing on a chair, fiddling with her diamond heart earrings, while Goutsou stood on the vault runway. On her first attempt, Goutsou took a step out of her landing, and her score was only 9.925, Nunno jumped again. Miller turned away.

One more chance for the gold, and Goutsou was ready. Her leap and flip were perfect. There was a small shake on the landing, but when the score flashed—a 9.950—Goutsou hugged herself.

"I felt very delighted," she said.

Before last night, Goutsou's participation in the all-around final was questionable. She had finished fourth on the Unified Team in the team competition, and only the top three from each team qualified for the all-around. But yesterday the Unified Team substituted Goutsou for Rosa Galieva, who was reported to have suffered a sudden knee injury.

Goutsou had played second fiddle to Svetlana Boguinskaia, a 19-year-old who barely knows her parents and who says she's afraid to quit gymnastics because she knows of nothing else to do with her life. Miller had been considered the second best in the United States ever since Kim Zmeskal won the world all-around championship in 1991.

But when last night's competition was over, after each of 36 girls had done optional routines on the uneven bars, in the vault, on the balance beam and in the floor exercise, Boguinskaia and Zmeskal were locked in a teary embrace in a corner of the Palau Sant Jordi, while Goutsou and Miller had disappeared into the depths of the hugs of their coaches.

Neither Goutsou nor Miller is very good with words. Goutsou used the phrase "thrilled and delighted" several times—at least that's what her interpreter said—and Miller is as uncomfortable expressing herself as a sumo wrestler would be tiptoeing across a balance beam.

But that was OK. To watch each perform almost flawlessly last night, with her face taut, her back straight as a ruler and her blue eyes focused on nothing but the piece of equipment on which she was competing, was to learn everything about the two stars.

Goutsou looked no prouder than when the pale blue and yellow flag of Ukraine was raised during the medal ceremony. In the women's team competition, Goutsou had been part of the Unified Team. But the International Olympic Committee is allowing Unified Team athletes to compete under the flags of individual republics. For the first time, the Ukrainian flag waved at the Olympics and the Ukrainian anthem was played.

"I felt very, very proud," Goutsou said. "Someday, I hope to compete for the Ukrainian team also."

Last night's competition was billed as a grudge match between Zmeskal, 16, and Boguinskaia. When Zmeskal won the world championship last year in Indianapolis, Boguinskaia groused that it was a home-town decision, that Zmeskal's routines weren't very difficult and that she hadn't performed them all that well either.

But it was clear last night that Boguinskaia's routines weren't all that difficult, either. Mary Lou Retton, the 1984 Olympic all-around champion, said that Boguinskaia was performing the same routines that won her a bronze medal at the 1988 Olympics.

"She does it well," Retton said, "but the other girls are doing more difficult tricks now."

Including Zmeskal. In the floor exercise, she is known for a spectacular tumbling pass that includes three straight backflips on which her hands never touch the ground. She had no trouble with that. It was when her feet touched the ground that she had trouble.

The floor exercise, her best event, was first for Zmeskal last night. It didn't bode well for her when she was left pacing on the mat while a judging dispute involving a previous competitor was heard. And when she landed after her last tumbling pass, her left foot touched down over the restraining line on the mat. That is an automatic deduction.

Zmeskal knew when she walked off that mat that her hopes of a medal were gone. After just one routine.

Afterward, Zmeskal, unable to contain her tears, took time to describe her disappointment. She had finished 10th. Betty Okino, also of the U.S. team, was 12th. And Boguinskaia was fifth.

"This wasn't the best evening of my life," Zmeskal said. "I just made a mistake at a bad time."

She was by herself because her coach, Bela Karolyi, who finds the spotlight when his gymnasts are winning, had disappeared from the gym before the medal ceremony.

It has been a horrible Olympics so far for Zmeskal. On her very first routine of the team competition, she fell off the balance beam. And she almost didn't make the all-around finals.

It has been a perfectly terrific Olympics for Miller, though. On April 1, she had surgery to put a pin in her left elbow to help heal a chipped bone. Nunno said that the injury might have been a blessing in disguise. Miller had to miss the world apparatus championships in Paris in April and the U.S. championships in May.

"All the pressure and attention was on Kim [Zmeskal]," Nunno said. "Shannon was just in the gym, practicing."

Now Miller has a chance to make history. She already has a bronze medal from the team competition and her all-around silver. Next up are the individual apparatus finals tomorrow, and Miller has qualified for all four events. No

Olympian ever has won six gymnastics medals.

"I think Shannon can do it," Nunno said. "I really do."

Miller smiled. No words were needed.

Observations on deadline writing

The worst brings out our best.

Death. Dishonor. Destruction.

Hurricanes, murders, executions.

Real deadline writing is the best it gets in newspaper journalism. It's when our juices really flow. The rush of words, the tumble of facts against the clock. And we always tell it better if it's awful.

This year's winner, Sam Stanton of *The Sacramento Bee,* didn't have a pretty story to tell. His description of the death by cyanide of convicted killer Robert Alton Harris was gripping. I found myself involuntarily gasping for breath as I read the story. Read this death scene:

> While other gas chamber victims have thrashed and fought the gas, Harris appeared to give himself up to it.
>
> He never clenched the arms of the chair to which he was strapped, and his muscular body moved in a slow, almost graceful response to the asphyxiation.

The Miami Herald's Marty Merzer, who received an honorable mention, is a reporter I've long admired. He doesn't get in the way of his story. A wise reporter, he lets the story tell itself. Read his lead on a Red Barber obit: "If baseball could speak, it would have sounded like Red Barber." His story on the tenth anniversary of the Vietnam Wall brought tears to my eyes. And his Hurricane-Andrew-is-coming story was terrifying.

These were some of the first entries I read. No smiles. Then, a sports story. Finally, something to cheer for.

Diane Pucin of *The Philadelphia Inquirer,* covering the Olympics, says about two women gymnasts: "They look like two strands of spaghetti, Tatiana Goutsou and Shannon Miller. Both are blond and pale, and they bend and curl and flutter as if they have no bones." Pucin was our other honorable mention.

And there were some good stories that didn't get prizes, such as Robert McFadden's *New York Times* story on the huge storm that paralyzed the East Coast in December. The storm roared through his story with a life of its own. McFadden's lead:

> Howling like Valkyries on a rampage, a huge prewinter storm packing gusts up to 90 miles an hour and enough rain to submerge a small state

struck the New York metropolitan region yesterday. It crippled transportation, commerce and education, flooded wide areas, knocked out power to hundreds of thousands of homes, damaged thousands of buildings and disrupted the lives of millions of people.

And the wonderful sentence from John Kass of the *Chicago Tribune* on some pols who got caught with their hands in the municipal cookie jar: "Politics is a carnivore's game, and weakness means opportunity."

I almost dismissed the Madonna interview story from the *Toronto Star* before I read it. I would have been wrong. It's a delightful piece that shows what you can do with a bored celeb interview. Reporter Peter Cheney captured it cleverly:

> It will be 20 minutes long. That's what you get. Exactly. And when your time is up, it's time to leave, whether you're satisfied or not. That's what it's like with Madonna. Her meter is running. There is no such thing as a freebie.

And with Julienne Gasseling of *The Alliance Times-Herald* in Nebraska, it wasn't even how well she wrote or any phrase she turned. It was the clarity of her copy considering how fast she had to write. I could feel her heart pounding as she ran back at the noon recess every day about 12:10 to make a 12:30 deadline, covering the biggest story in town, a gripping murder trial.

But we were surprised we didn't get more good entries. There were obvious holes. Where was the great stuff out of the Los Angeles riots? And from the mother of all deadline news, the Associated Press?

While we may have wished for more, we still read some terrific writing.

The one line that haunted me afterward was written by Wil Haywood of *The Boston Globe,* an account of his terrifying capture by Somali warlords: "There were bodies on the roadsides, eyes like marbles rolled to a stop."

Deborah Howell, Editor
Newhouse News Service

Dorothy Rabinowitz

Commentary

DOROTHY RABINOWITZ, 58, editorial page writer and television critic for *The Wall Street Journal,* won the ASNE Distinguished Writing Award for Commentary with her sharp-edged columns and previews.

Rabinowitz was born in Queens, New York. Queens College graduated her in 1956 with a baccalaureate degree in English. Rabinowitz freelanced for years around New York City. She later worked for the *New York Post* and for *New York Magazine.* She joined *The Wall Street Journal* in 1990.

Rabinowitz has little patience for the way she sees America and New York City going. She writes with enormous confidence from what she describes as a centrist conservative core. She has a very New York voice.

Congratulations, Dorothy. Keep talking.

On the Perot trail

JUNE 29, 1992

In election seasons as in all seasons, nothing quite energizes our journalists so much as the fear they may be accused of lacking investigative zeal and toughness. So the media have now gone into high gear on Ross Perot, currently the target of relentlessly intense—if also slightly muddled—revelations on the evening news. One report last week—a model of its kind—came from a reporter for WABC in New York covering not-quite-candidate Perot's address to a throng of Connecticut supporters.

It was clear, this journalist informed us, that this crowd wanted specifics and answers to Mr. Perot's stands on issues—and that it was no longer content to wait or accept generalities. In fact, something very different was clear about this scene. What was clear was that this crowd was busy shouting its head off for Mr. Perot. It was also clear that the reporter's observation was not a description of the crowd but a recital of the current litany—i.e., that the would-be candidate's lack of specifics and programs must soon undo him and his campaign.

We have been hearing this or versions thereof from the beginning of Mr. Perot's campaign. Hardly a day has gone by, certainly not a weekend, without some pundit promising that the voters would get to know Mr. Perot and find out Lord knows what, or reject him for his vagueness, or that he would say something or do something and it would all be over. With a single sentence his campaign could go poof!— the way George Romney's or other alleged sure-fire favorites' once had.

But nothing of the sort has happened to Mr. Perot. In fact, the more exposure he got, on *20/20,* on morning television and talking to David Frost, the more journalists began to grasp—

and in some cases appreciate—the reason for his appeal. A regular on *The Washington Week in Review* marveled at the amount of trouble he had tearing himself away from the set during Mr. Perot's two-hour performance on morning TV, while also noting his inclination to doze through Gov. Clinton's performance.

With the Perot bandwagon showing no real signs of slowing, TV news seems to have decided to turn the heat up. Heat, of course, is not the same as light. In some cases, the light shed reveals more about the journalism at work than about Mr. Perot. Take a report by NBC's Bob Kur, for example, which first announced that in Buffalo, N.Y., Perot support had "crested like a fad." Mr. Kur then proceeded to ask Perot supporters questions designed to elicit proof of their ignorance about the man. The reporter found an old man who admitted under questioning that he knew nothing of what business Mr. Perot was in or how he had made his money. Mr. Kur, apparently deeply shocked, repeated, "You don't know *how* he made his money?" till the abashed old man made his getaway. The reporter also found a couple of Perot supporters who weren't up on all the latest as regards their candidate's views —not exactly a new phenomenon among voters. Still, the picture drawn for us here suggests that something unique and possibly quite ominous is going on here, with benighted citizens forming up behind a mysterious candidate. The report ended with the undeniable—if vapid—observation that "the people Ross Perot has brought into the political system can just as easily step back out."

Perhaps, but it is also clear that a lot of Americans have fallen in love with Mr. Perot, and, contrary to rumor, falling out of love is hard to do overnight. It is true that in his TV appearance last week, Mr. Perot gave the first hint of tendencies that could accelerate the process. Pressed by Bryant Gumbel, who asked a well-put and pointed question about his

views on the Clinton-Sister Souljah contre-
temps, Mr. Perot waffled and babbled and
showed signs he can pander with the best of
them.

* * *

Journalists working the campaign trail are
still looking slightly giddy after a week spent
laughing it up over Dan Quayle's spelling adventures. Now it is true, very true, that a vice
president should know how to spell potato. On
the other hand, to hear TV news readers who
can barely get through two sentences without
committing some atrocious assault on the English language waxing superior over a misspelled
word is also slightly dizzying.

The same journalists who daily contaminate
the airwaves—and so have taught generations
of schoolchildren abominations on the order
of "between you and I"—aren't, between
you and me, in any position to laugh. We are
talking here about people who—with few ex-
ceptions—offer daily testimonials to their
primitive grasp of the language. These are people who talk, before open mikes, about the relationship between "he and myself" or "myself
and her," the myself craze having grown quite
out of control. One can't even argue that these
assaults on English are simply the expression
of free spirits unconstrained by stuffy rules.
The insistent misuse of "I" and "myself" represent nothing but misbegotten notions of genteel English.

The New York Times reports on 13-year-old
Amanda, winner of the 1992 spelling bee, who
shared her views on Dan Quayle's spelling er-
ror. In her view, Amanda told the reporter, the
vice president should have been able to spell
potato even though he "had some sort of flash
card he was reading the wrong spelling off of."
Right, Amanda. Maybe when you've rested up
from the spelling bee you can crack a grammar
book—or maybe just any book written before
1960—where you will find no off-ofs. But who
can blame Amanda, when the off-ofs fly out a

mile a minute from the TV set, which is of course where she heard it.

There is, of course, an occasional bright spot where one might not expect to find it. It turns out that one of the few people in broadcasting (not counting David Brinkley, Messrs. MacNeil and Lehrer and a few others) who knows the term is "more important" and not the appalling "more importantly" is a sportscaster. Tom Terrific Seaver. Perhaps in some future better life, networks will send their broadcast stars to spend a little time boning up on the mother tongue and maybe, if there's time, a little history. We are talking here about a public service that would be no small potatoes.

Observations and questions

1) Rabinowitz starts her piece with a general framing statement ("In election seasons...toughness.") and then moves to the anecdote from Connecticut. Rewrite her opening so as to lead with the anecdote. What would you gain in interest and lose in clarity?

2) The first paragraph has two asides: "—if also slightly muddled—" and "—a model of its kind—." Think about asides in terms of interrupting the flow of sentences versus creating a sense of conversation and thinking.

3) The second aside ("—a model of its kind—") says the opposite of what the author eventually means. List everything the phrase could mean and then think about how readers might interpret it. How can we use such irony without confusing readers?

4) The second paragraph uses the phrase "was clear" four times. How does the parallel structure created by this repetition help Rabinowitz make her point?

5) Rabinowitz closes the first section with praise for Bryant Gumbel as an interviewer and a jab at the politician, the reverse of her opening. Why does this switch make an effective ending to the section?

6) The second section flames with ferocious phrasing: "atrocious assault on the English language," "contaminate the airwaves," "taught generations of schoolchildren abominations," and "primitive grasp of the language." What picture emerges of the author from such wording?

7) Rabinowitz rages against what she sees as atrocities against the English language. Should journalists write and speak in strictly correct language, even old-fashioned correct language, or in the language of their readers and viewers? Why?

Welcome to Gotham

JULY 13, 1992

NEW YORK—To the Democrats: a hearty New York greeting. Be assured, you are in for some fun in the city known to the world as the Big Apple or—its more recent name—Calcutta by the Hudson. Most of you have been here before. But since in New York fun and fashions are eternally evolving things, here are some guidelines.

Don't assume, merely because you are on a sidewalk, that you are safe from motorized vehicles. It's not unusual for motorcyclists to bypass traffic by roaring onto the pedestrian walk. You'll want to keep an eye out for them, not to mention the menace of the speeding bicycles that will narrowly miss you—or maybe not. In recent years New Yorkers have come to understand that being on the sidewalk means they can at any time be cut down by the armies of delivery people from Domino's Pizza or Chinese take-out restaurants traveling at 70 miles an hour. So keep a sharp eye out and, where possible, consider using the streets, which many New Yorkers now consider safer than the sidewalks.

SOCIALLY ENLIGHTENED VALUES

Whether in the street or on the sidewalk, you will not avoid the blast of car stereos, or hand-held boomboxes, set at a volume that can be heard for 30 blocks. There is, as it happens, a law against this sort of thing in New York (as there is about vehicles on the sidewalk). But in a city like this, where socially enlightened values prevail, enforcing the law gets complicated. Just a few weeks ago, police who confiscated blaring boomboxes came under fire from a judge, who accused them of prejudice against minorities.

During your stay, you'll probably have need of taxis. If you are fortunate enough to find a driver who knows where Madison Square Garden is, don't expect calm acquiescence if you venture to tell him what route you prefer to take. For some drivers, such a request is enough to put you in the category of an oppressor—and to get you an embittered look at the very least. Or, the cabbie may simply announce he'll take you his way, just leave it to him.

New York cabbies are a sensitive lot, quick to take affront. Ask one to lower his radio a bit and he's likely to snap it off altogether and drive in belligerent silence the rest of the trip—a good outcome, on the whole. He may, on the other hand, tell you to get out of his cab. This happens a lot. Stay put and don't be cowed—unless the driver brandishes a weapon. To start your ride off right—and also prepare yourself for what's ahead—proffer a hearty "good morning" or "how are you?" when you get in the cab. If the driver doesn't answer, he's either in a sullen rage or—as is very likely—he doesn't know English. Either case requires your alertness. There are, of course, also cheerful, capable and courteous cab drivers working in New York. With luck you may find one.

If you want to try subways, you will find this is the fastest way to get around. To be sure, you may encounter—along with assorted other mendicants—persons whose piercing voices will rend the unquiet air of a subway car as they ask for everyone's attention. They are there, they will tell you, to solicit funds to buy shoes for homeless children and that they represent a charitable organization that is invariably nameless. Most New Yorkers have learned to keep right on reading their papers at such times.

If you haven't thought to bring a newspaper, there is plenty of other reading matter around, in the form of subway ads. One should say right off that these ads, which are largely directed to drug addicts, alcoholics, battered wives and such, don't make the most cheerful reading and may leave on a visitor the impression that New York is one large halfway house.

To receive such an impression, of course, it's not necessary to take a subway. In fact, riding a city bus can produce the same effect. For whatever reason, surface transportation attracts the highest concentrations of people who have divined that the CIA is controlling them by radio transmitters installed in their fillings. The numbers of these people wandering around are of course an excellent testimonial to the liberation drive that brought the mentally ill out of institutions and into the streets. Convention delegates have a first-rate opportunity to view the results of this piece of progressive social planning.

But you'll want some fun. Hop on a bus or whatever and ride down to Greenwich Village. Here you can see where Henry James lived and the Washington Square of which he wrote, where Walt Whitman, Edna St. Vincent Millay and Eleanor Roosevelt lived. Henry James would have been surprised, of course, at some of the sights now to be seen in his old neighborhood.

Today the handsome streets are lined with cars, and the cars all have signs in their windows, entreating thieves not to break in. They are pitiable sights, these invariably courteous —if not positively craven—messages informing would-be thieves, "Nothing left to steal. No radio. You've taken it all." Occasionally there is a slightly more dignified sign, i.e. the brusquely informative "No radio." And from time to time you can come across a message with a rare note of asperity, such as the one that read "You've broken in three times, don't do it again. Florida thanks New York." Notice how the tone trails off, from militance to mush, in that last line. All this elaborately pleading prose has been put forth on the assumption that the people smashing in car windows care what anyone writes about how many times they've been robbed.

Here in this neighborhood of expensive co-ops and townhouses, panhandlers stand five to a block. They are white, black and Hispanic or, as the mayor might say, part of the gorgeous mosaic. They are also pros, who put in a fair amount of daily travel time to get to their favorite corner. One husky 27-year-old, who commutes from New Jersey, will tell you that the best money comes when temperatures hover near zero, and he can huddle under a blanket. This can bring in $300 a week or more but, he attests, summer is rough. As soon as it gets hot, he says with disgust, New Yorkers walk right past you, and then everything depends on the tourists. Bear it in mind.

You may want to wander back uptown now and look around. Over on the far West Side, after you've seen the USS *Intrepid,* consider a visit to the Javits Center, which was built to house trade fairs. It is home, above all, to the annual auto show. The Javits Center may show autos, but don't try arriving there in one if you expect parking arrangements. The Javits Center, while splendid in other regards, is another one of those testimonials to progressive social planning. In this case the planning involved the concerns of environmentalists, who wanted fewer cars around.

In your travels you may notice large gatherings of people shouldering plastic garbage bags or with carts crowding into the entrances of large buildings. Do not mistake this for a homeless shelter or soup kitchen; more than likely you are looking at a supermarket. For, where once the clerks at Gristede's or D'Agostino concerned themselves with selling groceries, they are now much of the time busier directing the flow of traffic from people returning plastic bottles for deposit, and dealing with the fights and eruptions that ensue between deposit collectors. Push your way into the market anyway. You might want to pick up a bottle of soda or two, since what your hotel will charge you for a soft drink would be enough to buy lunch in the rest of the country.

THE ENTERPRISE ZONE

You may also notice, if you find your way to Fifth Avenue, that things don't look the way they used to around those once gleaming streets and fabulous shop windows. The reason is, of course, the line of peddlers hawking their wares on these same sidewalks. Like the bottle collectors, they are trying hard to make a living, and the place they have enterprisingly chosen is the environs around Tiffany's and Trump Tower.

Wander along, now, to the Garden, where things should be cheery and hopes high—at least for this week. If you're walking, remember—if you want to live—that before crossing a one-way street here you look in both directions. Welcome to the city. If you can make it here—especially across the street—you can make it anywhere.

Observations and questions

1) The column starts with a light tone and the notion of two New Yorks: "the Big Apple" versus "Calcutta by the Hudson." Study how Rabinowitz alternates the two New Yorks, and keeps her tone light even when saying devastating things.

2) In the third paragraph, Rabinowitz says: "But in a city like this, where socially enlightened values prevail, enforcing the law gets complicated." What does she mean by "socially enlightened values?" Do you have to agree with her values to understand what she means?

3) This column indirectly takes potshots at people who don't speak English, beggars, the mentally ill, victims of auto theft, people recycling bottles, and street peddlers. What kind of readers do you think Rabinowitz is addressing?

4) The *Journal* editors turned this passage into a pull-out: "Panhandlers stand five to a block. They are white, black and Hispanic or, as the mayor might say, part of the gorgeous mosaic. They are also pros." Is the paper an equal opportunity insulter, or ridiculing the mayor's liberal rhetoric? Or both?

5) Rabinowitz uses the second person form of address throughout, ostensibly aimed at the prospective visitors. Who is the real "you" in this piece?

6) Rabinowitz closes with an allusion to a hit song by Frank Sinatra: "If you can make it here—especially across the street—you can make it anywhere." Besides its subject, New York City, what relevance can you see for this reference?

Love him tender: Our Elvis obsession

AUGUST 10, 1992

Are you lonesome tonight? Hold on till Wednesday (10-11 p.m. on CBS), at which time *48 Hours* will introduce you to people who are also lonesome and who know what to do about it, which is to think about Elvis. The program—which has the richly suggestive title "Crazy About Elvis"—was spawned in honor of the 15th anniversary of the singer's death. Dan Rather, who introduces this piece of Americana with impeccable delicacy, observes, with only the barest hint of wryness, that 8% of Americans aren't even sure Elvis is dead.

He *is* dead, Mr. Rather firmly notes. That may seem an obvious fact, but—this being a political season in which definitive stands on hot social issues are as rare as a hound dog's teeth—it behooves us to appreciate forthrightness wherever we may find it.

Toward the end of the program, Mr. Rather also delivers one of the few poll results of recent weeks that won't be alarming to George Bush—unless things are worse at the White House than they seem. According to this *48 Hours* poll, 44% of Americans count themselves fans of Elvis Presley.

Intrepidly genial and respectful, the program's crew of reporters get Presley's devotees to talk—not a hard thing to do, admittedly—about what Elvis is to them and why they want to go and cover all the walls and ceilings of their houses with Elvis pictures and make 18 pilgrimages to Graceland, as some of the grandmotherly women interviewed here have done.

Still, why not? Americans have had no real pop-culture hero in some time, in the past few years no political one either. Clearly, Ross Perot was the new American Elvis, but then he rudely went away. The original Elvis, at least, was concerned about his fans, so much so, some of those fans think—and say—that he faked his own death to spare them the torment of watching him grow old. Greater love hath no man. Indeed, as one ardent traveler to Graceland—a woman with 12 grandchildren— says, the existence of a higher power may be open to question, but Elvis is as close to being one as there is.

Not all of his devotees hold views of Elvis that are—comparatively speaking—so moderate as this. But it's clear from the outset that in doing what they do they all have fun—fun, it's true, that is heavily laced with mournfulness, and that clanks around at memorials and grave sites. They do, on the other hand, also make pilgrimages to Elvis's birthplace in Tupelo, Miss., a two-room bungalow on a small patch of grounds lovingly sculptured and tended. In this segment, reporter Phil Jones listens soberly to the news—delivered by the shrine's official historian—that Elvis was born at 4:35 in the morning on Jan. 8, 1935. About 500 couples a year come here to get married at the shrine's chapel, we learn.

The first segment introduces Betty Buddy and three female friends, preparing to make one of their frequent journeys to Graceland, sounding for all the world like frenetically happy teenagers. They are of course not teen-agers, but grandmothers and great-grandmothers now, but in a significant way still the people they once were, the young who once screamed their lungs out for Elvis. The footage of Elvis mania shows frenzied fans looking exactly like those who earlier swooned for Frank Sinatra. The Voice, who had the most extraordinary career run in memory, is fortunately still around, but even if he had departed at Elvis's relatively tender age, it's hard to imagine throngs of his devoted fans invading Hoboken for years to come, or doting on reports that Frank is still alive and hiding out in a Holiday Inn in Guam or Irkutsk or wherever. One possible reason for the difference is that Presley's fans, unlike those of Mr. Sinatra, seem to have come up in an era not only comfortable with the aberrational but, indeed, devoted to it.

Here we get to see the ceilings and walls covered with Elvis's visage, to hear reporter Richard Schlesinger coyly ask the owner if it mightn't be a bit too much maybe—and the proudly delivered inevitable reply that there is no such thing as too much Elvis. One woman sweeps into her bank and demands her safe-deposit box, which holds, not jewels, but her autographed picture of Elvis. None of the segments is more fascinating, or funnier, than Bill Geist's travels in Vegas among the Elvis imitators. It is, of course, much easier to poke fun at some Vegas hulk with dyed sideburns waxing earnest about his Elvis career than at a bunch of grandmothers. Some of the grandmothers, it turns out, have developed a secondary mania for Elvis impersonators. Elvis mania, it appears, is a train with no stops. In chasing it, the *48 Hours* crew brings us a perfectly splendid ride.

* * *

Almost the same might be said about another piece of Americana, to be delivered next Monday on HBO (9:30-10:30 p.m.) and titled, *Never Say Die: The Pursuit of Eternal Youth.* This dour survey of efforts to hold off the inevitable does, it is true, pause for a brief look at the elderly disporting themselves in Baden-Baden, but for the rest, film maker Antony Thomas provides a strictly American assortment of dupes, dopes and cynics. Too bad Mr. Thomas did not employ a lighter-handed, less moralistic treatment of his subjects. After all, when you have taped a cosmetic surgeon talking about himself with deadly earnest grandiosity, the way the one here does, no underlinings are required. You will meet here the life-extension folk, and the cryonics advocates who freeze you into immortality for a price, and lots more. Finally, Mr. Thomas takes us to France and two happily wrinkled grandparents, to show how wise and right it is to forget efforts to fight aging—another smugly platitudinous moral. By now one expects Polonius to appear to tell us, "To thine own self be true." For all that, Mr. Thomas has made a sharp, if not very cheering, film.

Observations and questions

1) This piece on Elvis Presley has three allusions to The King's songs, all at the top: "Love Him Tender," "Are you lonesome tonight," and "hound dog." Would the piece improve if the author sprinkled more such references throughout? Why?

2) This *pre*view, as opposed to a *re*view, has to describe programs the readers have not seen. How can a previewer explain things without spoiling the future experience for readers and viewers?

3) This piece satirizes Americans' devotion, indeed mania, for Elvis, without implicating the readers. Study how Rabinowitz aligns her readers with her as outside this craze.

4) In the second half, Rabinowitz complains about Anthony Thomas, the filmmaker: "Too bad Mr. Thomas did not employ a lighter-handed, less moralistic treatment of his subjects." How does Rabinowitz avoid the appearance of heavy-handed moralism in her own piece?

5) Each of the two sections ends with brief and qualified praise for an upcoming television program. People interested in the subjects will watch no matter what she says. But how does she encourage the general viewer, if there is such a person, to watch the programs?

6) This preview treats two unrelated subjects, and Rabinowitz has placed them end to end with a transition sentence as a bridge: "Almost the same might be said about...." Would it help the reader to have a lead that ties the two subjects together, and perhaps an ending that echoes the beginning?

Talk show McCampaign comes to end

NOVEMBER 2, 1992

The final (one can only hope) all-star talk fest of this remarkable election season took place Friday night when David Frost interviewed the three candidates. The show also produced the best opening line of the season. As George Bush settled into his chair, Mr. Frost asked, "Well Mr. President—had a busy day disrupting weddings?" A small thing perhaps, but that small ripple of tart abandon had a decidedly tonic effect on ears exposed to long weeks—months—of reverent formalities from television interviewers talking to presidential aspirants. The morning and evening show hosts have much of the time pursued their inquiries with the delicacy of combatants making their way through a minefield—the reason being, needless to say, their unwillingness to pursue questions in a way that would encourage candidates to go off and make news on somebody else's show.

Who can forget Larry King last week, ("No no, Ross, I just meant," etc.) placating an increasingly hostile Ross Perot who looked as though he might just get up and leave if Larry didn't stop trying to get him to say a little something about the famous wedding plot. Two weeks earlier, the *Today* show's perky and sparkly Katie Couric not only got a White House tour with Barbara Bush, but also the gift of an impromptu on-camera visit with the president himself. It was, by current standards, a journalistic coup of sorts if not very newsworthy—not the sort of opportunity that would be extended say, to Dan Rather, who has been excluded from all interviews with Mr. Bush as payment for their on-air tangle in the last election.

That said, it remains true that one of the chief fascinations of this election is that so much of the campaign is taking place on TV talk shows in soft interviews. Despite much solemn brooding over this issue, and concerns that the candidates are escaping hard scrutiny and turning the campaign into TV entertainment, it's clear that the voters have—as a result of this exposure—a tremendously keen sense of the campaign, and the campaigners. That is of course precisely what is upsetting them. Americans tuned in to the debates in such astounding numbers because they were searching for some reason to justify a vote for any one of the three candidates. Not for nothing did Americans become presidential debate junkies overnight. They were on a hunt—one that became a fascination. That fascination is now turning desolate for the large numbers of voters, and they *are* large—who still can discover no reason to vote for any of the candidates, and for whom the prospect of a Bill Clinton as president and four more years of George Bush are equally unimaginable.

For better and worse—and much of the latter—the public got a view of the candidates that only the relaxed flow of soft talk show exchange would allow. A candidate peppered by questions in a formal debate, or a hard ball interview of course reveals much about himself, including especially his capacity to absorb and regurgitate the research and position papers prepared by his staff. But the candidate basking in the bonhomie of prime time talk fests ends up revealing himself in more profound ways—as these candidates did. The conversations with David Frost showed the process at its clearest. Here was George Bush happy the poll gap was closing, happier still to be at the end of the trail, and talking in those slightly daffy circumlocutions that characterized the earlier days of the campaign. Asked by a gently probing interviewer whether America was, as he had promised to help make it, a kinder, gentler place than it was four years ago, the president said that it *was* kinder and gentler in some ways.

Now that will, of course come as no small
surprise to citizens who have seen the growth
of a criminal violence unthinkable even a few
years back, and who have seen the brutal ram-
page of thugs in the Los Angeles riots. But as
we soon saw, Mr. Bush was indeed able to discern a lack of kindness and gentleness in
American society—though one having nothing
to do with the abovementioned realities of life.
What it had to do with—as he told Mr. Frost
with deep and genuine passion, was the toughness of the election campaign: Never had he
seen one so ugly and harsh. Such is the depth
of the president's focus on the world outside
his political campaign.

True, it has been a long campaign and the candidate is tired. It is also true that this campaign
was notable for the extraordinary absence—both
in the debates and journalistic inquiries—of the
gut issue of crime. The Clinton campaign's master strategists had their famous sign reminding
themselves to stay with their chosen focus i.e.
"It's the economy, Stupid." And *everybody*, including journalists, obeyed.

Next came Mr. Perot, a witty fellow but
clearly in no mood for Mr. Frost's introductory
joke. Mr. Perot gave a wintry little smile, upon
hearing how William F. Buckley had said,
when running for mayor in 1965, that, should
he win, he'd call for a recount. Mr. Perot then
proceeded to recite—yet again—that he was
running at the behest of the people, for the
children, for you name it and that he intended
to win. Bill Clinton was on his best linguistic
behavior this time, suppressing the Ozark reflex that had this Rhodes scholar telling Larry
King last week, that the Republicans treat people "like it don't matter." Did he regret not
serving in the war, Mr. Frost asked. He regret-
ted the whole thing, the war, everything, came
the politic and decidedly vague answer. He
was, Mr. Clinton said, proud, very proud, he
had done what he thought was right. Mr. Frost
kindly neglected to point out that this is not a

very compelling argument, considering the number of villains who could make the same claim. Finally, Mr. Clinton proved he was generously endowed with the '60s generation's extraordinary sense of its own historic importance. His election, he told David Frost, would served to unite a nation still divided by the Vietnam War.

No, there is hardly any doubt: The television talk shows have done their job presenting the candidates these many months. The question is whether we can ever forgive them for doing so, and whether we can, knowing all we know, drag ourselves to the polls.

Observations and questions

1) The first (long) paragraph has complicated sentences expressing complex ideas in twisty (even turny) ways. We seem to experience the author thinking in front of us, and we expect the rest of the piece to unfold in an equally complicated way. Should we start complex pieces in simple ways to stabilize readers, or should we push them headlong into the torrents?

2) Simplify this sentence: "The morning and evening show hosts have much of the time pursued their inquiries with the delicacy of combatants making their way through a minefield—the reason being, needless to say, their unwillingness to pursue questions in a way that would encourage candidates to go off and make news on somebody else's show." What does your simpler version gain and lose?

3) The point of this column comes in the third paragraph: "Despite...campaigners." Rewrite the point sentence and make it the lead. Would this revision make the first two paragraphs ("The final...last election.") easier to follow?

4) The first three questions suggest making this complex piece more accessible to general readers. But the author says she does not write for general readers, and the changes would undermine her writing voice. Think about the role of special preserves in the newspaper to serve specific audiences and to showcase style.

5) Consider this sentence: "Bill Clinton was on his best linguistic behavior this time, suppressing the Ozark reflex that had this Rhodes scholar telling Larry King last week, that the Republicans treat people 'like it don't matter.'" What values and attitudes can you discern underlying this sentence, especially the phrase "Ozark reflex"?

6) Readers remember most whatever they read last. If they get to the end of this column, they will remember this last sentence: "The question is...whether we can, knowing all we know, drag ourselves to the polls?" Re-examine the whole piece to see how Rabinowitz expresses her world-weariness without turning off the reader.

The 'good book' on prime time

DECEMBER 14, 1992

Hide the school-age children and call out the American Civil Liberties Union and the People for the American Way. The Bible is coming to television, right out in public where everyone can see and hear it—or, anyway, that version of it to be aired on Arts & Entertainment for four nights beginning Sunday (8-9 p.m., EST).

Now, after the public schools have had to banish every whisper of anything that could conceivably be construed as religious influence, commercial television comes along with a program like this—with Charlton Heston reciting from the Old and New Testaments at the River Jordan, in the Sinai, Old Jerusalem, Jericho and other places famous in Holy Writ and from newspaper coverage of the modern Middle East.

This week the Good Book is on prime time, but only a few days ago, officials of Vienna, Va., decided that the town's choral society could not include "Joy to the World" or "Silent Night" or any other carol mentioning the birth of Jesus at the Community Center's annual Christmas program. The Vienna town officials, it appears, were cowed by the possibility of a lawsuit from the ACLU. The ACLU, as all the world knows, labors night into morning at this time of year, to save the nation from Nativity scenes. As George Orwell said—and as it keeps being necessary to repeat—there are some spectacles before which Satire herself stands mute.

The Bible program begins at the beginning, with Mr. Heston—aglow in torchlight—reciting from Genesis in the Roman Amphitheater at Beit She'an, Israel. It's hard not to think on what that recitation sounds like to contemporary ears, and especially to the legions now majoring in what is known as "Women's Studies" —a population now busy learning the sacred writ on the evil of "patriarchal" traditions. Thinking on that does add a certain *frisson* to the experience of listening to the archetypally (splendidly so) patriarchal Mr. Heston read from Genesis about how Eve was made from Adam's rib to be man's helpmate, and how she was tempted by the serpent, ate of the apple and brought about the Fall of (dare one say it?) Mankind.

Feminist scholars have long been busy, of course, bringing new and progressive perspectives to such subjects. Only a week or so ago, National Public Radio broadcast the views of one such expert, who explained that the pantheon of women heroes goes all the way back to Eve. It was only natural that Eve had dealings with a serpent, this analyst informed us, since serpents have long been known to have healing powers, and women have always been healers.

It should be said at once that the program, titled, appropriately enough, "Charlton Heston Presents the Bible," succeeds smashingly on most counts. Those include, one should also say, its spiritual and religious dimensions. One has to stop and say that because of the thick set of production notes distributed to the press, jampacked with assurances that this series—whose subject is the Bible (King James version)—really doesn't have much to do with religion.

A specimen of the times and their cultural terrors if ever there was one, these notes include nervous explanations from executive producer Fraser Heston (the star's son) that "This project is not about religion, it's about literature, art and history." Charlton Heston himself feels compelled to say that this is an acting project and that he is not "guided by any doctrine nor seeking any evangelical purpose, not converting or educating...." On and on this extraordinary document continues, with director

Tony Westman putting in that he was not raised in a religious household—but he knows now that the Bible is a great book whether one believes in it or not.

With the creators squeaking in this way to ward off the culture police, it's something of a wonder that they managed to produce the series at all—much less the one that emerges. What emerges is a work steeped in religion and spiritual passion.

It is not, in short, a film about art or even literature. The great religious works of Michelangelo, Rembrandt, Masaccio, Raphael, Blake, Bosch and the others that appear here are, in a literal sense, the background: They are not the point. The art is also meant, of course, to illustrate the spiritual mainsprings of Western culture, something the film does very well indeed.

It is Charlton Heston, of course, who brings the whole thing together—who struts around in a wide-brimmed Western hat perusing the desert horizon and saying things like "and there was that business with the apple." (Eve, he meant.) Mr. Heston serves up his own biblical redactions and commentary. He earned the right to do this with hard work—crossing the Jordan on foot, traversing Israel and filming the holy places from Jericho to the Sea of Galilee.

In May, the relentlessly modish production notes say, a "multicultural" crew started location filming. Five weeks later, this rainbow team returned with the goods, with such awe-inspiring shots as Mr. Heston atop what's left of Jericho, announcing that beneath him lies "23 layers of civilization." He describes such scenes as "Bible performances"—an apt term. And they are far from easy, these performances through which he seems to glide so persuasively. It takes a certain effrontery—the sort of actor's effrontery Charlton Heston has always had—to stalk about the desert and holy places with the assurance he shows here, reciting from the Scriptures and telling of Abraham and

Moses and Christ and the Flood. An impressive accomplishment all told. It's nice, especially, to think of all the products of today's education system who might end up watching this history—much of which will doubtless come as big news to them.

* * *

Just What Everyone Is Dying to Know Award for Distinguished Journalism: Our broadcast journalism citation this month goes to NBC's Katie Couric—the handsdown winner for on-air coverage the morning U.S. troops landed in Somalia to begin famine-relief efforts. After first inquiring about the troops' rations she went on to ask the big one: Would the *press*, would the members of the *media* in Somalia, Ms. Couric worriedly asked, have enough nourishing food to eat?

Congratulations, Katie, for addressing an anxiety we know must haunt the minds of all Americans at this hour in our history.

Observations and questions

1) Rabinowitz does not think of herself as writing leads, but the first paragraph turns into one. How does this paragraph set a tone, predict the content, and orient the reader for what follows?

2) The author keeps evoking Charlton Heston without describing him or his career. Look at each instance and describe what she assumes readers know about Heston. How can journalists estimate what their readers know about public figures?

3) In the third paragraph, Rabinowitz says: "The ACLU, *as all the world knows,* labors night into morning at this time of year, to save the nation from Nativity scenes." [My italics.] What does she mean by "as all the world knows"? Think about how this clause defines the author, her intended audience, and everybody else. Including you.

4) In the fourth paragraph, Rabinowitz says: "Thinking on that does add a certain *frisson* to the experience of listening to the archetypally (splendidly so) patriarchal Mr. Heston read from Genesis about how Eve was made from Adam's rib to be man's helpmate, and how she was tempted by the serpent, ate of the apple and brought about the Fall of (dare one say it?) Mankind." Think about how this passage (with its parenthetical asides) sets up her attack on feminist scholars in the next paragraph.

5) What does *frisson* mean? How can journalists gauge what words their readers know? How can we use words our readers don't know in such a way that they will understand anyway? Do columnists have a license to use trickier vocabularies?

6) In the middle of the piece, the author satirizes the "thick set of production notes distributed to the press" with the preview tape. Watch how she separates her attack on the surrounding political correctness from her very real appreciation of the television program. We think of framing devices as enclosing things, but they also separate them.

A conversation with
Dorothy Rabinowitz

DON FRY: Who taught you to write?

DOROTHY RABINOWITZ: I learned from reading. I was reading Thomas Mann when I was a very young person. And later on, Henry James taught me to write.

That famous teacher and editor.

That's right: Henry James and Rebecca West. When you read people like that, it's very hard to get them out of your prose. I grew up in an era when school was different, and teachers were different, and it mattered.

I grew up in the same era, born in 1937.

Ah, then you know.

What's it like to work for *The Wall Street Journal*?

It's a civilized and marvelous place, with friendship and conviviality and the freedom to say what you wish without anyone stopping you. That was new to me, because, outside of *Commentary,* someone was always cutting, or changing my sentences around, or changing the political tone of them.

Actually, *The Wall Street Journal* is famous for heavy editing of an enlightened sort.

Nobody, nobody touches what I write. Nobody!

[*Editor's Note: I have heavily edited and rearranged this conversation for brevity and clarity, and recomposed the questions.*]

Your writing is not edited at all?

Of course, it's edited occasionally. I write editorials, and of course, that's a kind of joint effort, and you understand that somebody puts a
paragraph in. But in my television columns, no
one ever changes things politically by saying,
"You don't want to offend X, Y, or Z." And I
have written in many, many magazines (which
shall go nameless) where something happens to
your prose. It gets heavily rewritten for all
manner of reasons.

**Alas. Tell me about your editorial board
meetings.**

We just sit down, very informal, and we exchange bouts of hysterical and uncontrolled
laughter at everything. I say, "Guess what lu-
nacy I just saw. This person has been defecat-
ing on the streets, and he has been appointed
the Fire Commissioner," or something like
that. And they say, "Well, yeah, you should
write an editorial about that."

Sounds like fun.

The last thing I wrote was about *Bartlett's
Familiar Quotations.* Justin Kaplan, the editor
of *Bartlett's,* did a new edition in which he decided to leave out everything significant that
Ronald Reagan ever said, and put in the most
absurd, deathless quotes from James Earl
Carter, and that's the sort of thing I tend to
write.

Do you take assignments?

Oh, absolutely. At *The Journal,* of course, it
comes in very genteel form, and one can certainly refuse: "How would you like to write...?"
And, of course, it's always something wonderful that has been thought up for you. I write

about one editorial a week now. You don't have to sign your name; that's nice. [Laughter]

How would you characterize the political stance of your editorial board?

As you probably have guessed, I don't know a lot about economics, but *they* are centrists. They're what used to be 1950s liberals.

Hmmmmm.

Of course, today a 1950s liberal is considered a conservative.

Right, right.

They're very, very leery of hard-right conservatives, and they're sort of worried about Pat Buchanan, and they're not very fond of him. And neither am I.

Good for you. And do you identify with their views?

Oh, yes.

That makes it easy, doesn't it?

Look, everything you see, entertainment and everything, if you watch television, is produced by a certain political culture, and to have this view helps me to understand what I'm seeing on television.

Right. Where do your ideas come from?

If you have a question, you tend to find yourself bringing it up, or testing it to see how people feel about it. Among one's friends, among your writing friends, you say, "Did you see X, Y, and Z?" They say, "God, you ought to write about that." And I say, "Right. Right." That's

it. The one test I have is that you have to be
excited. You know that.

I do. I write in white heat.

You cannot have a neutral feeling and just write
the column.

**So you try things out on your non-journalist
friends.**

All of my friends are all sort of New York neoconservatives: Midge Decter, one or two others, and the male person in my life to whom I
am not married. You know, at this age, and
indeed for the past 20 years, they're sort of fel-
lows of your soul, and you trust their reactions. And if someone were to say to me, "I
don't think that's very interesting," I would pay
attention.

Do you try ideas out on your editors?

Yes.

Are they good at it?

Not always. My editor has completely different
interests, but he listens. He's considerably to
the left of me, although not very much, I
mean, not by normal standards.

Right. Right.

But he certainly has a deep core of liberal sen-
sibility which I do not have. But the wonderful
thing about him is that he cares about writing.

And the others?

My other colleagues, oh, yes, yes. That's what
nourishes you here. You need a family, you
need a kind of intellectual, political family.

What does that "family" do for you?

It tells you you're not alone, especially if you have grown up in another time. We are living in a generational wartime...

You bet!

...and I feel like one of the killers on my side, and I'm happy to be. The one time our core atmosphere failed was during the Los Angeles riots. A terrible, terrible, bleak depression hit everybody, so no one could talk, and everybody sort of went home, but that's rare.

Where else do your ideas come from?

Reading the paper. Sometimes I read the wire services. But most of the time, you just walk down the street. For example, "Welcome to Gotham" is the product of my daily walks on the street with my dog, Rudolph Rabinowitz. This is in your bones, and this is part of everybody who lives in New York. Everything you feel can be turned..., *is* turned into something.

I bet you have personal crusades....

Yes. I want to preserve the English language from its destruction, and the erasure of history in anything on television, or the rewriting of history in prime-time television. Everything on television reveals the imprimatur of someone trying, for the best of possible reasons (which are quite disgraceful), to rewrite and change the facts of history.

And political correctness is a real crusade. I praise the powers that be who preserved me from a life on the campuses. I mean, I could be the queen of the English department in Palmyra, New Jersey, now...

Aren't you glad you're not!

(That's right.)...discussing feminist literature. There are people of intelligence and culture who are now forced to teach rot. We are watching the decline of a culture, and we have front-row seats. But I don't give up. Anybody who has grown up in the '40s, in the wartime years, has this feeling that if you try and try, you're going to win.

Now you've told me what you're crusading *against*. What are you crusading *for*?

Something bad has happened to our culture (which is a wonderful culture). I'm crusading for the return of certain pristine values: merit, reading, literacy, civility, that sort of thing, the return of our culture.

Are you winning?

No. But you cannot lie down. You cannot say that generations that come after you are worse than the ones you knew. They have been mistaught, and you have to fight. The core of the problem is the education system. If I walk into a university bookstore, I see row after row after row of absurd, minor women novelists instead of Henry James and Willa Cather, and that's what's wrong.

Who are your readers?

To write well, you should have a reader in your mind, and I have a circle of friends. I have the writer Midge Decter, my editor Bob Bartley, Norman Podhoretz, and an Australian friend of mine in Washington, Owen Harries, the former ambassador. And all of these people I have grown up with, who used to be neoconservatives, but who simply wrote for *Commentary* and thought the same thing. And others, the editor of *New York Magazine,* Ed Kosner, who knows what's right and wrong.

Hmmmmm. So you aim at this circle of friends?

I don't aim at it. No, that's not what I aim at. These are the people I feel looking over my shoulder. My aim is towards nameless figures out there who think what I think, and I speak for them. I know they agree from the volume of my mail, and the passion and the literacy of this mail. And every time I write a piece about what television reporters do to the English language, I get the most extraordinary, eloquent mail from all over the country, and the most beautifully written letters.

Can you characterize those nameless figures?

They are literate, highly literate, and they are crushed by the culture. I feel like someone who is speaking for another time, and I would hate to see that in print, but that's true. I feel that....

Wait, stop. Why would you hate to see that in print? That's what you stand for.

I suppose so. Because it sounds so very grandiose, but it is true nonetheless. I feel that we're swimming away into the most degrading kind of loss of cultural moorings. PBS did a program a couple of weeks ago called *Renaissance*. Renaissance! They had Martin Luther, and then they had Betty Friedan on! They brought in contemporaries who were supposed to be equal to the Renaissance. And I thought, "Serious professors of the Renaissance had something to do with making this film, and they produced *this*?" And I remembered what Kenneth Clark did in his *Civilization* series years back, and I thought, "This is how the culture has changed. You can't even trust a PBS audience to watch something on the Renaissance, but you have to bring in every jerk who has ever rebelled for some dumb reason and make him a kind of figure of the Reformation." And this happens night after night on television.

Galileo meets Susan Brownmiller.

That's what happened! They had Galileo and Betty Friedan, and I could not believe this. And I wrote about it, and I poked fun at it. We always say here: "What if we didn't have this place to vent our feelings?" I write it, I feel terrific. I say, "The hell with you, you fool! This is what you have done." And I really mean it.

The rule of writing is you cannot be polite, but you must be civil. You cannot be crude, but you cannot take prisoners either. And there is just too much of that middling stuff going on. Satire is everything.

Right. When you write irony and sarcasm, how do you keep from going over the edge so that readers reject you?

Well, it's a very important question, very important indeed, because I am often repulsed by grossness. I have read all my life and have absorbed, and I now understand the delicacy of the stiletto thrust. The reader will understand. There's an old Hebrew proverb: "He who understands will understand." At this paper, you are writing to an audience of people who *do* understand. I have yet to get a nasty letter in my three years here, and that's saying a lot.

You allude constantly to culture and books. If your attitude is "He who understands will understand," don't those references shut out a lot of other readers?

That's right. Very often, our copy editor will ask, "What does this mean?" I say, "Never mind, that's a line by Frost." At the same time, it shocks me that she doesn't know that line by Robert Frost.

But you want her to question it.

Yes, I want her to question it. And they're very nice about it. They say, "Oh." Now they don't ask anymore when something doesn't make sense to them. They figure it's a line of poetry. I do it....

Stop. Stop. Does it help you that they don't ask anymore?

No. It doesn't bother me one way or another. They figure somebody out there is going to understand it.

Yipe!

And I try not to make absurd references. It comes out on the page, and somehow it seems absolutely right.

So you don't think of yourself as writing for the general reader at all?

I do. I think the general....

Now wait a minute, wait a minute. You can't say, "They figure somebody out there is going to understand it," and still write for the general reader.

No one has ever called to say, "I don't know what you're talking about." I think the general reader is going to live with an allusion, or he will look it up, or he will ask. By now, the column has a following. In a sense, it's waving the flag of the literary and cultural values for which I hope we all stand. I do not change my sentences for the general reader. I think they're pretty plain-spoken most of the time.

Hmmmmmmmmm. I find them quite clear, but I'm trained as an English scholar, so I share your world of reference.

Yes. But I think that the others will say, "Well, who knows what she means? Let's go find something else."

Well..., okay. How do you organize your pieces?

I've been doing it the same way always, and there is one thing no editor has ever had to complain about: No one has ever had to shift a paragraph around. They just begin where they're supposed to. I unconsciously organize things like a court brief.

Aha, as an argument.

I am presenting a case. Whether the case is "This is a wonderful television program," or "This is an act of the most extraordinary deception," I'm making a case.

How do you start your case?

I have pieces of paper lying around the house, and if I'm really agitated about something, I start writing it, and I insert a paragraph at the proper place somewhere. That may turn out to be the core of rage, or the core of irritation, or whatever.

You write in longhand?

I do. I wake up at night around midnight, before the column deadline, and I sit and cover a legal pad for a few hours. You don't stop and fiddle with the prose that way, and you can keep your flow going. Then I sit down before the computer, and I take that scribbled garbage (and it is garbage), and I just rewrite it. By then, I have much assurance because something is down.

You rewrite it as you type it into the computer.

That's right, and really rewrite it, because then you can see. There's nothing like seeing on a screen.

Exactly.

I try to get the last sentence clear in my mind, so I know where I'm going.

Before you write?

Yes. In the first place, it's a wonderful reassurance. You know what it's like: You're tired at the end, and God, by that time, who can think of a sentence? But it's also a kind of lighthouse, just as the first line is. If you know the first line of a piece five hours before you write it, you've got that piece written.

I usually know the gist of the first sentence and the last, and I just connect them.

That's right. And the last line too, especially if you're being epigrammatic, shapes your thinking. But it helps to take your time a bit, and I never leave time, and I am very bad at that, very bad.

So you know what you're going to say before you say it.

Oh, yes. Not in detail, but I know the tone of it. Of course, it's true that you discover what you're going to say along the way, but you certainly know the point of it.

But there are some moments, and they're very frequent, which I marvel at. A deadline is coming, and you're taking it easy, and you *don't* get that usual crushing gloom, which I always get before writing, which everybody I know gets. And then you find out why: because it's all there. It has written itself in some unconscious way, and you knew you had it.

What causes that "crushing gloom"?

No matter how long you've been writing, and no matter how assured you are (and I'm very assured now), writing is not life. Life is having fun; writing is not fun. I know there are people who sing when they write, but writing is fun *when it's over.* It depends on who you are as a writer. You remember that 19th-century rule of writing: Load every rift with ore. Whether you choose to or not, if that is the kind of writer you are, writing is not fun. Every line has to matter.

And every word.

Every word. Every line has to advance. You have to pack it, and you have to make every sentence as good as it can be. Now that's hard, and that's why you get the crushing gloom.

How do you know when it's good enough?

You know. Oh, you know, because you can't leave it alone if it's not. I think there ought to be a happy medium where you can say, "All right. I'm never going to get that line any better, or that thought any better." But I can't seem to do that. If you have these extraordinary standards for every line, you're going to be fighting a lot.

Word by word.

Now I know why people drink when they write, or why so many writers turn to drink.

Maybe they're trying to get their internal demon drunk.

It *is* a demon. I experience it as a demon.

You should see *my* demon, a huge one with fangs and red eyes! Do you revise as you go

along, or do you write the whole thing and then revise?

Oh, no. I revise every line as I go along. First, when I'm scribbling along on that yellow pad, I don't do any revision; but when I'm at that computer, I see those deadly sentences with the emptiness at their heart.

How did your piece about Perot come about?

Watching that debate, and thinking as I was watching in front of the television set, as though I were talking to a friend in the room. There's so much political talk among our friends. I have very close friends, and we sit there and say, "Did you see that? Did you see that?" And I do a lot of that. I have a friend, Elizabeth Hodge, who watches with an even colder eye, and a cold eye is crucial. And you're watching in a different way from people who are not writing about this. But mostly what animates it is the impulse to upend the prevailing view, which can be false and foolish and absurd.

How do you begin pieces?

The first time you feel you're saying what you want to say, that's when the piece starts. There's a lot of tap-dancing around the point, and I often throw away everything.

Do you tend to write the "tap-dancing," and then cut it out, or do you go directly to the heart?

I don't want to have that tap-dancing, and it's always a sign to me of trouble. It's a sign to me that that paragraph should be thrown away, and there's some deception I'm perpetrating on myself. I have noticed that if there is any kind of blocking, it's for some social or political reason, and it's not for any other reason. Even if you have a head cold, if you have the flu, you can write. But with a serious inhibition, there's some subject you don't want to really discuss. Also there is tap-dancing if you don't have a strong enough grip on a really important thing that you think you want to say.

Does the tap-dancing help you grip it?

Yes. I think it helps to show you that you're not at the right spot, and then you go back, and you say, "What was it that made me interested in this? Why did I pick this topic?" And if you have to, you go for a walk with the dog or something, but get back to that lucid, white-hot point that made you connect.

And then you cut out the tap-dancing.

Absolutely. And then you start again, and you get into it and start moving. One of the things I've learned to do when I'm feeling very low, where I don't have that internal grip, is to take that yellow pad and start writing anywhere, and see where it's taking you. And that's the act of discovery. And all of a sudden, you find yourself writing eight pages. You say, "This must be important."

Writing by discovery....

That's right. And I discover all this, and I say, "My, God, this is the core of the piece. Forget all the rest of it." Something is telling you what's important.

And it has to do with your mood too. If you're really feeling gay and cheerful and full of abandon, and driven that way by a subject, you have a different kind of beginning. But if you're feeling bowed by the weight of centuries, that's there too.

Listen to the first sentence of your Perot piece: "In election seasons as in all seasons, nothing

quite energizes our journalists so much as the fear they may be accused of lacking investigative zeal and toughness." Does that sentence apply to you?

Oh, no! Oh, heavens, no. No. This is one of the things I have against our investigative journalists: their uncontrolled and highly selective zealotry, especially during election season. It is this very phony value, to see themselves as the guardians of our culture. They are, in large part (not all), but in large part lacking in so many of the virtues. To watch them believe in investigative zeal as an important principle is laughable to me, and this is the post-Watergate craziness they all feel. It's the moralizing.

Yes.

It's easy to stick a camera in somebody's face, and terrorize some clerk, and then turn around, and that's what they do all the time. Mike Wallace does it at a high level. Now, where did this come from, this investigative zeal and toughness? Journalists have to investigate, and they must be truthful, and they must be unrelenting in their pursuit, but that is not the principle of journalism. Journalism is supposed to inform. And I certainly don't identify with that.

Okay. In the second half of this piece, you blast the misuse of the language, one of your crusades. How did *you* get so good with the language?

Reading Henry James. It's reading. It's growing up in our time. You know, who on earth goes about saying "between you and I" except the products of teachers who were brought up in the 1960s. It's absolutely astonishing to me. And I got mail on this piece from editors of newspapers who regaled me with what reporters on their staffs had written, people who feel the same way about this.

Our language is slipping out from under us.

It is slipping out. And language is the culture.

Yes. Exactly. The "Talk Show" piece typifies your style: long complicated sentences and lots of asides. Those asides create a sense of conversation with your readers.

Asides are everything. The readers are the other people who are sitting watching, and you couldn't help seeing how good Clinton was at this stuff. Life does get easier for writers as you get on with it, in the sense that you have one thing that makes you confident that you didn't have when you were 25 years younger: You can make something of this; you are not going to say anything boring, or you wouldn't have picked the subject.

Yes.

And it may indeed be really boring in the world, but the person who should not be bored, and cannot be bored, is you, you the writer, or you'll get nowhere.

Let me read you the last paragraph: "No, there is hardly any doubt: The television talk shows have done their job presenting the candidates these many months. The question is whether we can ever forgive them for doing so, and whether we can, knowing all we know, drag ourselves to the polls." You just said you must not bore yourself, but you seem terribly weary in that last paragraph.

That's right. You're weary about what you're saying, not bored with the election. I felt this is the way people feel, and I am one of the people, and I am one of the people who cannot drag myself to the polls. And I thought that this was an unusual..., unusually open expression for me of..., instead of resentment and instead of (What shall I call it?). Instead of anything else, sarcasm, it's an expression of a dilemma.

This is your most sincere piece.

Well, it was. It was sincere in the sense of not being quite as nasty. What you properly call "weariness" is a kind of despair. How on earth could we have arrived at this state where these two bloody mediocrities are our presidential candidates? And that was very real feeling driving that. And I would normally have cut, and I would normally have made something much tarter.

What happened that made you so direct here?

The feeling of genuine horror, the real.... Is this the best we can whelp up? All your real emotions rise to the surface. You're not quite the repressed self you were, and this is the..., the real feeling of depression that..., that this is who is here. And I still feel it; I feel it much more now than before.

Because Bill Clinton won the election?

I look at the president, he's up there every day, and I cannot look at him, and I cannot look at his wife, and I have never had that experience, of being unable to look at the elected President of the United States.

When you do look, what do you see?

Everything I loathe culturally, everything, everything, everything!!!

Uh-oh.

Murray Kempton said that his hair rises on the back of his head in horror when he even hears the name "Clinton." It's his piety, it's his...,

his looseness, it's his flabby..., flabby sincerity, and it's his views. It's his lack of grounding in any center of gravity I recognize. It's his boyishness, not the Kennedy boyishness; but it's the little boy boyishness of the..., of the.... One could go on.

Yes, you could. Is it the man or his generation?

I think it's both. But there are lots and lots of other people of that generation, including members of his political part of the spectrum, that would not produce this in me. I found Jimmy Carter an awful president, but I was fascinated with him.

He has become a great ex-president.

That's right. I had no trouble looking at Jimmy Carter or listening to him. He was intelligent; he knew things. But I hope this goes away.

Well, four more years. For you. We talked about your despair with the way things are going and the generational problems. How do you keep going?

The joy of battle! I look back upon Iwo Jima and all those great battles of my childhood, and the flag going up on Mount Suribachi. My whole life is lived culturally somewhere inside the Second World War.

So is mine.

The walls of my bedroom are full of those pictures, and documentaries and tapes. We grew up in a nourishing time. We lived in the best of the century. I believe in Americans, I do really believe in them. I believe in the sense of the American people. If I have a religion, my religion is America, in a way. And I believe that they will come round, but the fight has to continue, no matter what it takes. So, yes, I think that what keeps you going is the real zest of battle. I do not sit around and say, "This is the way it is now." No, I say, "We lost what we were, and we're going to preserve our culture, so long as I breathe."

To preserve that culture, you're going to have to incorporate a whole lot of new people who aren't like you.

That's right.

Have you ever thought of expanding your audience a little?

Well, I don't know the answer to that, except to say I never do think of that audience. I say these things, and people come round to it, and they really are a vast variety.

You see, the schools have refused to recognize how much people want to learn. People aren't just brought up to watch MTV. They know something is missing in their lives, or they're ready to recognize something else. They're ready to grow up. There are a lot of people who share my views.

Maybe lots of writers out there believe as you do, but they don't write with your precision. How can they start saying what they really mean?

They have to connect with inner passion and be literate. To really learn, at whatever age, to read. There is a thing that's called the structure of an English sentence, and balance, and rhythm, none of which anyone can teach you except by reading. And if you have gone to college in these times, and if you've learned that Kurt Vonnegut is about as high as literature can aspire, you're in a lot of trouble. But there is this vast world of literature out there, and you sit down and read, and read, and see what it is to strike out far with a metaphor and a simile, and to have a responsibility in a sentence, and the challenge of making (What shall I say?) a sentence sing with meaning instead of letting it drop.

There is so much fatigue in writing. There is so much flab, and there is so much indulgence, and there is so much self-reference. I mean, the first thing I would do is force everybody to remove the word "I" from their process. I..., I don't believe I've written the word "I" in 25 years except when I was forced to do it in *Harper's*. But the omniscient observer, the kind of authority to write an authoritative sentence....

Dorothy, it's easy to be an omniscient observer, if you're Henry James. But I think writers who want to say what they mean may not have the nerve to be omniscient observers.

That's right, and you need nerve. And how do you get nerve? Passion, real passion! I don't mean flighty passion, I don't mean political passion, I mean you have to connect with a sense that something you have to say is of overweening importance. That is your authority.

I was once teaching somewhere in the Bronx, starving as a graduate student, in a very low state, and I went to this candy store, and this elderly woman said to another woman, "Have I got something to tell you!" And I leaned over instinctively, and I thought, "That's what writing is: Have I got something to tell you!"

[*Editor's Note: I respect Dorothy Rabinowitz as a person and a writer, and for this well-deserved prize. But winners of this award tend to become models for other writers, so I must dispute her dismissal of copyediting: "Now they don't ask anymore when something doesn't make sense to them."*]

Clayton Hardiman

Finalist, Commentary

Clayton Hardiman attended Michigan State University and Western Michigan University, graduating in 1972. At the *Chronicle* since then, he has served as a reporter, editor, and now columnist. Hardiman also publishes poems and short fiction in literary magazines. The National Association of Black Journalists and the National Society for Newspaper Columnists have honored his work.

His column reprinted here represents a black man paying tribute to the courage, intelligence, and beauty of black women. He also teaches his readers a lesson in perceptions, some shared and some tragically unshared.

Pictures bring wonder, celebration

JUNE 19, 1992

The curve of Wilma Rudolph's neck. The vicious joy in Earnestine Anderson's grin. The humility of Autherine Lucy in her simple go-to-meeting dress.

I am in the company of women.

Rosa Parks stands in church, her hands resting on the back of a pew. My mind tells me she is posing for a photographer, but my soul tells me she is listening to God.

Ruby Dee is wrapped in a shawl and standing on a manhole cover on an unremarkable street. She looks for all the world like the proverbial woman on a pedestal—but that proverbial woman is no match for her.

I am with these women in the Muskegon Museum of Art. The exhibit is photographer Brian Lanker's I Dream a World: Portraits of Black Women Who Changed America.

The photographs are black and white. They play hide-and-seek with light and shadow. The women in the photographs warm the cold marble walls.

They are athletes. An impression of speed persists in Wilma Rudolph's stillness. Althea Gibson is strong and victorious in her elegant black dress.

They are writers. Alice Walker leans a little to one side, as if she had caught sight of something interesting only to have you block her view. Sonia Sanchez cradles her wide forehead in one hand as if calming the fires there.

They are leaders and doers. Former Congresswoman Barbara Jordan occupies her wheelchair like a judge on the bench. Midwife Josephine Riley Matthews' weary head rests against the high back of a rocking chair, her white hair a nimbus cloud.

They are actresses, sculptors, musicians, historians. Each face is a history recital; each body angle a raucous blues. Some of these women look regal, some strong, and some at peace. Some are just tired and looking to rest.

Cicely Tyson's eyes are mournful; baby's breath mists round her head. Angela Davis sits in a tree, her dreadlocks remindful of its branches.

What do I think about when I look at these women?

I think about a small black-skinned girl who prayed that God would make her look more like the white actresses she saw deified each night on TV.

I think about a black-skinned woman whose husband called her ugly and wondered aloud why he ever married her, punctuating verbal blows with physical ones.

I think about women I have seen, listened to, known. I search these walls for my wife, my mother, my sisters and friends. And I see them, even though their photos aren't here.

I think about the skirmishes I've seen black women and men fight—love, anger and self-loathing in a rugged, bitter blend. The women expressing rage with words and body language, the men with blows and absence.

I think about how this museum should be filled with people, both sexes, all colors. But above all, there should be black men here, a crowd of us, with barely enough room to move. Wondering, celebrating.

I am blinking when I emerge an hour later on the street. My eyes won't focus, my brain refuses to adjust. The sun is out, which amazes me. It should be night right now. A clear night, with stars and a precise crescent moon.

Five or six young black men have just walked past, laughing and talking, and now they are about two-thirds of a block away. I feel like calling after them. Wait a minute. You got to check this out.

But I don't, mainly because I know what they'd see if they looked back. They would see a wild man on the sidewalk, yelling as if he'd lost his mind. Talking about print dresses and vicious smiles and misty, luminous eyes. In broad daylight, it would seem ridiculous. To the sane mind, it would probably make no sense.

THE SUN

Roger Simon

Finalist, Commentary

Like Richard Aregood, Roger Simon had won the ASNE Distinguished Writing Award twice before, a feat only four people have managed. The other two are Greta Tilley for non-deadline, and Sam Francis for editorials. Simon has a B.A. in English from Illinois, and he worked at the Danville (Ill.) *Commercial-News*, the Waukegan (Ill.) *News-Sun*, and *City News* in Chicago. He has a roomful of prizes.

Simon's cold eye and hot prose miss nothing in his piece about George Bush slogging to defeat in the last days of his last campaign.

Bush is no quitter, Atwater realized in 1980 campaign

NOVEMBER 2, 1992

CHIPPEWA FALLS, Wis.—The gunmetal gray sky hung lower and lower all day until, as the light faded over the flat farmland, it seemed to touch the shoulders of George Bush.

He stood on the little caboose platform of his 19-car campaign train, coughing into his fist and reading each carefully-scripted attack on his opponent from notecards that riffled in the wind.

Hoarse and blowing his nose into a white handkerchief, only one thought seems to sustain him: Win or lose, this will be it for him.

Win or lose, he will never have to campaign again, never have to ask for a vote, never have to beg the people to give his life meaning.

Win or lose, he will soon be free.

And this is what gives him comfort in these last hours. It is so delightful a thought, in fact, that he said this day: "I can hardly believe it."

I cannot tell you with certainty whether George Bush will win or lose. But I can tell you that if he does win, many on his own staff will be very surprised.

Even with all the balloons, all the fireworks, all the cheerleaders and bands, George Bush's last whistlestop trip had all the zest and high spirits of the train that carried Abe Lincoln's body from Washington to Illinois.

And notwithstanding the souped-up, sound-bite rhetoric that his staff cooked up for him before each stop—"Being attacked on character by Governor Clinton is like being called ugly by a frog!"—Bush seemed dead behind the eyes.

He has been running for president, after all, for a very long time.

He began in 1980, running against Ronald Reagan for the Republican nomination. Bush beat Reagan in Iowa, but Reagan beat him in New Hampshire and continued to beat him around the country.

Even though Bush went on to win Michigan, there was no way he could beat Reagan. But George Bush would not drop out of the race.

Lee Atwater, who later would work for Bush, was then working for Reagan. "We kept beating him and beating him and he just kept hanging in and hanging in," Atwater said later. "That's when I learned something about George Bush."

What he learned is this: Whatever else his failings, the guy is no quitter. You give him the ball and he'll carry it. You write him the lines and he'll deliver them.

"He's afraid of the power he has lusted for!" Bush said this day in Wisconsin. "Governor Clinton over the last 24 hours has been frantically flopping around like a bass on the side of the Arkansas River."

Bush claims that he, himself, has never entertained a moment's thought about the possibility of his own defeat. And perhaps that is true. If there is anything politicians possess besides ambition it is an almost limitless capacity for self-delusion.

"Momentum," Bush would tell his press corps every day in 1980. "We've got the Big Mo. This ain't over until the fat lady sings."

And she sang in a voice loud enough for Bush to hear only when Jim Baker came to him and told him he was shutting down the campaign, that going on was pointless and, perhaps, if Bush maintained some shred of dignity he might be in line for vice president.

Where Bush then simmered for eight years.

And when he ran for the presidency in 1988, he almost blew it. Bob Dole and Pat Robertson beat him in Iowa, and if Bush had not won in New Hampshire, it would have been all over.

The polls were bad, the press was bad, even the weather was bad. But Bush hung in. And in the small gymnasium of Kingswood Regional

Junior High in Wolfeboro, N.H., Bush gave
what I came to call his "Vote for Me or I'll Kill
Myself" speech.

"I don't have to do this," he said, a catch in
his voice. "I'm 63 years old. I've got some
years of mileage on me and a few lines. But I'm
not done yet! I'm not done yet doing the work
of the people!"

And now, four years later, when everything
seems to be slipping away from him again, he
has returned to the formula that worked
before.

"This hasn't been a pleasant year," he tells
the crowds these days. "I've taken a lot of
shots from the media, from Clinton and Gore.
And people ask me, why do you need this? I'll
tell you why. I don't *need* the job, but I *want*
the job. I want to finish the job. And lemme
tell you, I finish what I start!"

Maybe. But only if the people let him.

Observations on commentary

A distinct clear voice that uses precise, descriptive, and skillfully-crafted prose to hold your attention from beginning to end, that's what good columns are made of. Commentary should be thought-provoking, producing profound responses from the readers. Some columns might engender outrage, some anger, some even tears. Others might cast a familiar issue in an entirely new light.

A typical column makes an argument, the facts marshalled to support the writer's point. At times, they can be narratives filled with nostalgic remembrances that emotionally place readers at the scene, reminding them of good and bad times past. Some of the most successful columns produce a lightheartedness, a temporary interlude from the unrelenting focus on the evils of our society that too often forms the context of news.

Acel Moore
The Philadelphia Inquirer

Richard Aregood

Editorial Writing

RICHARD AREGOOD, 50, editorial page editor of the *Philadelphia Daily News,* has won his third ASNE Distinguished Writing Award for Editorial Writing, a record. He probably would have won this third prize earlier, but ASNE made him a judge in the contest and therefore ineligible to enter.

Aregood was born in Camden, New Jersey. He is married to Kathleen Shea, television critic for the *Daily News.* He received a B.A. in English and political science from Rutgers in 1965. He joined the *Philadelphia Daily News* in 1966.

Richard Aregood never blinks. Deeply American in his thinking, emotion, and allegiances, he resists powerful people who want to distort the U.S. Constitution for their own purposes. He always says exactly what he means, and he seems to have more fun saying it than anybody else in journalism.

Congratulations again, Richard.

Does this stuff really matter?

JANUARY 28, 1992

The country's going to financial hell in a hand-basket. People who describe what's happening as a depression are starting to look like optimists. The world is changing faster than anybody can follow.

The president is waiting for somebody to tell him what will win re-election so he can develop a few heartfelt principles. The opposition is an as-yet-unformed band of people with broad political and philosophical differences.

It is a challenging time to be a citizen.

So what is being defined as the major issue?

We are supposed to care greatly whether Arkansas Gov. Bill Clinton got into a sexual tangle with somebody named Gennifer (with a "G") back when. She has told a newspaper that usually reports Elvis sightings and births of three-headed piglets that he did, and the "respectable" press is baying after all the details.

Clinton even went on *60 Minutes* to undergo questioning. This certifies the question as important, since only serious things are discussed on *60 Minutes*.

The whose exercise demeans Clinton, his wife and the questioner, as well as anyone who happened to be watching because they were still stupefied by what seemed like three days of Pepsi commercials interrupted by bursts of football. Only Mrs. Clinton's outburst of honesty, in which she effectively said the past details of her marriage were nobody's business but hers and her husband's, had even a trace of dignity.

Nobody seems to care that this is an important presidential election. Clinton isn't even being asked the kind of hard questions he should have to answer. Instead of being challenged on his vague, Southern strategy kind of message, he's being asked innumerable irrelevancies. Instead of being forced to put up a real program instead of sounding like a better-coiffed version of Jimmy Carter and George Bush, he's being asked everything just short of "Was it good for you?"

Speaking of Bush, he hasn't yet presented a plan or shown that he has a clue. That's after having been president for almost four years.

In fact, the only people who seem to be taking the campaign seriously enough to actually speak to issues are Democrats who have been decreed to have no chance. It would do more good for Americans to give some thought to the ideas of Paul Tsongas or Tom Harkin or Jerry Brown than it would for us to learn conclusively whether the governor was involved when Lulubelle did Little Rock.

So here's a little voter's guide. The fair Gennifer's story is full of lies. She was paid very well to tell it. No one will ever know the truth. But Clinton has pretty well acknowledged that he has been less than faithful in the past. The details are both irrelevant and none of our business.

If it matters to you, vote against him.

If it isn't the most important qualification for the presidency in your mind (and FDR would tend to bolster your argument), make sure you find out just what he does have as a presidential candidate. Find out whether he's just another sloganeer like the incumbent Education President. If he fails that test, it won't matter either way if he does it with donkeys.

And while we're at it, let's make sure we find out a few things about the other candidates, even the president who's currently lurching around looking for a reason for his candidacy.

All those people slogging around in the New Hampshire snow want a big, important job. We should find out whether we want to give it to them. If sexual probity is the only issue, let's elect Mother Teresa by acclamation, and spare ourselves the sound bites.

Otherwise, let's grow up and pay attention. Our inattention is part of the reason we're in the fix we're in.

Observations and questions

1) Aregood distinguishes two kinds of press: "She has told a newspaper that usually reports Elvis sightings and births of three-headed piglets that he did, and the 're-spectable' press is baying after all the details." Would you include supermarket tabloids in "the press"? Or does the distinction have any meaning in an era of blurred lines between information and entertainment?

2) The seventh paragraph ("The whole exercise...trace of dignity.") has an indirect crack at the Super Bowl in the middle. What effects does Aregood achieve by mixing the serious and the silly? What does football have to do with the Clintons' marital defense?

3) Aregood alludes to various happenings in American culture and history without explaining them, for example: "Southern strategy," "FDR," and "Education President." What can we assume our readers know, and how much do we have to explain?

4) Aregood leaps far beyond the bounds of good taste with references like "Was it good for you?" "Lulubelle did Little Rock," and "if he does it with donkeys." How much latitude can (and should) a "family newspaper" give its opinion writers? What good does the author accomplish with these cracks?

5) This author has a way of poking through the blather with simple advice to citizens, for example: "If it matters to you, vote against him." Look through all five of these editorials to find such instances. Notice where in the structure of the piece Aregood places them.

6) At the very end, Aregood turns from blaming politicians, the government, TV, and journalists for the country's problems, and points directly at the reader, at you: "Otherwise, let's grow up and pay attention. *Our* inattention is part of the reason *we're* in the fix *we're* in." Study all the preceding passages that set up this twist.

Punish crime—not ideas

MARCH 31, 1992

People who have never had an idea tend to have the same response whenever they're confronted by something they don't like.

They blame ideas. They especially blame the expression of ideas.

In this era of pinhead reasoning, a cottage industry has arisen. Stern censors, ablaze with the same righteous fervor such people have always had, have taken on new protective coloration.

Many are masquerading as feminist scholars, especially in law schools. Possessed with the quaint notion that you can eliminate crime by preventing people from thinking about it, they have come up with a seemingly endless series of censorship schemes, each pretending to somehow protect women. Predictably enough, they have found allies among anti-feminist, male, right-wing politicians, who have never met an idea they wouldn't censor.

Their current hobby horse is Senate Bill 1521, the "Pornography Victims' Compensation Act," which would allow victims of sex crimes to sue publishers for damages in civil court. There would not be any need to prove a crime in criminal court, just a series of vague requirements that plaintiffs show that material published or sold was a "substantial cause" of the not-necessarily-proven crime.

Before you get any weird ideas, this is not an attempt to justify sex crimes, crimes against children or crimes of violence. People who do such crimes should be as severely punished as the law allows.

But *they* should be punished, not some publisher who's reprinted Faulkner and is now confronted with an allegation that reading a book inspired some creep to do something loathsome.

As novelist John Irving wrote in an eloquent essay in the *New York Times Book Review* on Sunday, there was plenty of crime—even creepy sex crime—well before the invention of movable type, let alone the videocassette. Some people are violent creeps, with or without guidebooks.

There is always the impulse among many people to ban what they don't like. Everything from Mark Twain to Terry Southern to the feminist *Our Bodies, Our Selves* has been the subject of witch-hunters. The sexually explicit does not have much of a public constituency, so it is frequently a target.

But it is downright simple-minded to think a series of lawyer-enriching suits against publishers and booksellers is going to end murder and rape. Irving quotes Teller, the magician-comedian: "Advocates of this bill seem to think that if we stop showing rape in movies people will stop committing it in real life. Anthropologists call this 'magical thinking.' It's the same impulse that makes people stick pins in voodoo dolls, hoping to cripple an enemy. It feels logical, but it does not work.... It's a death knell for creativity, too. Start punishing make-believe, and those gifted with imagination will stop sharing it."

In fact, the one test that makes clear that all this is about is censorship is the lack of sympathy to Sen. Howard Metzenbaum's ironic suggestion that the bill might be expanded to cover the liquor and firearms industry. Do not hold your breath until the phony scholars come up with a legal-sounding way to do that.

There remains one good old-fashioned way to punish crimes like rape and murder. We put rapists and murderers on trial, convict them and put them in prison, thus punishing the person responsible for the crime. We do not go back and file a civil action against, say, Charles Manson's mother, for mistreating him and assertedly making him a monster.

But what, you might ask, do we do about pornography? We don't buy it, that's what.

More importantly, since today's climate is much more influenced by television than it is by all the pornographers on earth, we stop watching all the pant and snort and shoot epics on TV and we stop buying the products that are hawked on such shows. Maybe we even stop watching the TV news and thus become a little less frightened.

We use our rights without taking anyone else's. And all of us win.

Observations and questions

1) The first sentence looks simple, but isn't. Rewrite this lead sentence so readers can't stumble on it. What have you gained and lost?

2) In paragraph six, Aregood pulls back: "Before you get any weird ideas, this is not an attempt to justify sex crimes, crimes against children or crimes of violence." Why would the readers get such a "weird idea"? Writers who take risks have to anticipate and channel ideas that might pop into their readers' heads. Study how Aregood does just that.

3) In the middle, Aregood restates his lead: "There is always the impulse among many people to ban what they don't like." Why does he repeat himself? With what effects?

4) Divide this editorial into parts. Study what techniques Aregood uses on each side of the boundaries so readers know he has changed subject. Simple transitions work best.

5) Who is the audience of this piece? How can you tell?

6) This editorial refers to William Faulkner, John Irving, the *New York Times Book Review,* Mark Twain, Terry Southern, and *Our Bodies, Our Selves,* all in three paragraphs. How much cultural literacy can we assume on the part of our readers?

7) Three sentences from the end, Aregood says, "Maybe we even stop watching the TV news and thus become a little less frightened." Is this sentence a cheap shot or central to his argument? Why?

8) The editorial ends, after 14 paragraphs of torrential language and tricky sentences: "We use our rights without taking anyone else's. And all of us win." Make your point in simple sentences for maximum punch.

Frighten the horses?
No, the brass

NOVEMBER 13, 1992

About a hundred years ago, Mrs. Patrick Campbell uttered the wise words that we Americans have had trouble hearing ever since.

"My dear," she said dismissively, "I don't care what they do as long as they don't do it in the street and frighten the horses."

In our country, just the knowledge that they do it at all frightens many, including the chairman of the Joint Chiefs of Staff, the estimable Gen. Colin L. Powell, who doesn't otherwise appear to be a man who's easily scared.

Relax, general. It's not exactly a threat to life as we know it that President-elect Clinton plans to keep his pledge to stop discrimination against gays and lesbians in the military. It won't change many lives, other than those of the victims of that discrimination.

The General Accounting Office estimates that the services spend at least $27 million a year ferreting out people they can charge with being homosexuals. The military thus provides the double loss to the taxpayers of wasting all that money, then tossing out service people it has trained at great expense, often people who are doing a good job. It makes those $600 toilet seats look like chump change.

Opponents of ending discrimination in the military are considerably more subtle than the yahoos who write electoral initiatives like the recent one in Oregon.

"It is difficult in a military setting," Gen. Powell testified before Congress, "where there is no privacy, where you don't get choice of association, where you don't get choice of where you live, to introduce a group of individuals who are proud, brave, loyal, good Americans but who favor a homosexual lifestyle."

All due respect, general, but a lot of that sounds like the rationale given for keeping the Army segregated racially until President Harry Truman cut though the crap and ordered it done.

What olive drab fantasies is the army entertaining? Leather bars at Fort Sill? Marching drag queens at Fort Polk?

Except for those raving degenerate (and straight) fighter pilots at Tailhook conventions, it would seem that a soldier's sexual propensities are remarkably irrelevant to ability to do the job.

Nobody cares about you or your "lifestyle" in the army. The army determines the "lifestyle," and you, by God, live it.

Are the general and those who think like him saying they have no faith in the ability of officers and non-commissioned officers to maintain order? If it isn't already banned, it shouldn't be too difficult to enforce a rule against overt sexual behavior in the barracks.

Maybe they could expand the rule to cover NCO clubs and protect a few straight women from the jerk "lifestyle" the army doesn't seem worried about.

The army survived for hundreds of years without banning homosexuals. It has survived for the last 50 tolerating the dedication, bravery and perhaps even the existence of gay and lesbian servicepeople—as long as they were willing to endure the fear of exposure and instant dismissal.

The army will survive gays and lesbians who are proud and unafraid, just as well.

Who knows, it might even *improve* life in the barracks. Anybody who's had to listen to the cacophony of country music and rap with which youthful soldiers pummel anybody in earshot, might be grateful for the occasional show tune.

Relax, general. Our new president plans to do something that's right.

Observations and questions

1) Aregood leads with the horse quip by Mrs. Patrick Campbell. What does she mean? What does the anecdote mean? Why does the author lead with it instead of a more direct statement of theme?

2) The third paragraph begins: "In our country, just the knowledge that they do it at all frightens many." Who are "they"? What is the "it" they're doing? Who are the "many"? Why doesn't Aregood write more specifically?

3) Aregood directly addresses General Colin Powell, chairman of the Joint Chiefs of Staff. But who are the real target and audience(s) of this editorial?

4) In the tenth paragraph, Aregood attacks "those raving degenerate (and straight) fighter pilots at Tailhook conventions." Is this attack fair? Do editorials have to balance their arguments and meet fairness standards?

5) This editorial satirizes a mindset rather than debating the issue of gays and lesbians in the military. Would shifting the focus from General Powell to societal norms help or harm Aregood's argument?

6) The ending of the piece descends into light-hearted irony on popular music. Why is such a turn appropriate?

Those names on the long black wall

NOVEMBER 16, 1992

It started as a class project. She got a "B."

Undeterred, Maya Lin entered her design in the competition for the memorial for those killed in Vietnam. She won, and helped to heal a nation.

Not bad, considering that the "B"-giving professor was an also-ran in the competition.

After 10 years, the starkness and beauty of her design seem to grow, even though war-lovers insisted on inserting a flagpole and, later, a more traditional piece in which three soldiers stand to one side and look appropriately bewildered. No clutter can lessen the power of those names on that black wall—more than 59,000 people dead.

Perhaps that's the big thing Maya Lin did. This is a unique war memorial because it is for the individual lives given and taken, not for some dime novelist's view of combat glory. We all have a chance to remember them, pay them tribute and cry for them—and for ourselves.

Except for campaign season, when it's guaranteed that some sleaze-monger somewhere will grope for an issue, Vietnam memories are softer now. Part of that is the passage of time, of course, but much of it is the direct result of Maya Lin's magnificent art.

When you walk into her overwhelming sculpture, it doesn't matter what your opinions were about Vietnam. All those names and all that heroic lost youth take the politics away. It's a place where the old rigidities fall away.

It's a place where the old roll back the clock and struggle with the loss of sacrificed children...where the middle-aged become young and very sad...where the young become children and remember fathers who are long dead.

It's a place where we can finally grasp that wars are not just chapters in history books, that real people die real deaths by the tens of thousands.

A great mythology has grown up around Vietnam, based on the assumption that people who oppose the country they love doing something murderously stupid are somehow disloyal. It's a dangerous myth, but it's been pretty well weakened by Maya Lin's wall.

Those young men and women died for an extension of national policy, for a projection of power into an opposing sphere of influence, for loyalty to an ally so that the United States would not be perceived as a pitiful, helpless giant.

Or they died because of a crack-brained colonial war that was a mistake from beginning to end.

The flowers and flags and other adornments placed at the wall every day tell another story. It's more important.

Young men and women died for something, whatever it was.

We at home still mourn them.

Every one of us.

Observations and questions

1) Aregood leads with the irony of the designer of the Wall getting a B on it as a class project and then winning the design competition over her professor. Evaluate this anecdote as the opening of a sad commentary on one of America's most tragic events.

2) This editorial about the Vietnam Memorial never describes the monument itself. Why not? Would the piece have more punch if Aregood described "the Wall"?

3) Paragraph four ("After 10 years...people dead.") attacks America's usual way of memorializing wars. Identify the real targets here, beyond mere statuary.

4) Locate all the parallelism in this editorial, for example, "It's a place where...." What effects does Aregood achieve with this device?

5) Throughout this piece, the author plays two ways of thinking against each other, without describing either one. Would his argument improve from more precision? Why? What would he lose?

6) At the end of the editorial, Aregood poses several alternative interpretations for the Vietnam War:

> Those young men and women died for an extension of national policy, for a projection of power into an opposing sphere of influence, for loyalty to an ally so that the United States would not be perceived as a pitiful, helpless giant.
>
> Or they died because of a crack-brained colonial war that was a mistake from beginning to end. . . .
>
> Young men and women died for something, whatever it was.

Aregood moves from the language of military hype ("projection of power") to his usual direct savagery ("crack-brained") to inarticulate imprecision ("something"). How will readers interpret and react to that sequence?

7) Aregood's ending returns to the notion in the fifth paragraph: "We all have a chance to remember them, pay them tribute and cry for them—and for ourselves." Notice how simply he implicates the reader in this tragedy.

Bush pardoned six— and himself

DECEMBER 29, 1992

Great. Now we've got the criminals forgiving themselves. Even Richard Nixon, the Prince of Darkness himself, had the good taste to find some poor boob to blow out the charges against him.

Too chancy for a sleaze like George Bush. Or maybe he knew that Bill Clinton wasn't likely to indulge himself in self-destructive stupidity like honest but dim Gerry Ford was.

It was as if Nicky Scarfo, aglow with the holiday spirit and aware that hardly anybody pays attention to the news on Christmas Eve, had had the power to drop charges against a bunch of his hit men before they could rat him out.

That statement contains about the nicest thing you can now say about George Bush. At least he didn't have the witnesses against him terminated with extreme prejudice. That's Washington for whacked.

Forget about all the crap the Reaganisti are spreading around about Iran-contra. Bush said the case against former Secretary of Defense Caspar Weinberger, arrogant liar Elliot Abrams and the others amounted to the "criminalization of policy differences."

The fact is the policy was a criminal policy, administered in secret by criminals. This is a lot more than an ideological difference of opinion over a regulation.

These guys—Ronald Reagan, George Bush and those who are freshly pardoned—decided that the law and the Constitution were inconvenient to them. They decided that the balance of power in our government should be eliminated in favor of an all-powerful strongman who can do anything he wants. They decided that our president should not be hampered by messy democracy, that he should have absolute power, like Saddam Hussein or George III.

As always, Bush gives the lie to his own words about the grand principle behind his pardons. He didn't stand up before the election and state his position boldly. He waited until any backlash wouldn't matter to his own future and sneakily made his move.

He and this un-American band of conspirators have dragged this matter out for years—lying, destroying documents, concealing or withholding others, delaying, obfuscating and attacking the prosecutor, an old-fashioned, Constitution-believing distinguished Republican lawyer who believes no man is above the law. Then they complain that the investigation is taking too long and costing too much.

These men are not patriots, no matter how many flags they wrap themselves in. You cannot be a patriot while believing this great nation should ignore its own greatness and its own laws and behave like some homicidal junta.

For two decades, we have mostly been ruled by men for whom the American Way is nothing more than a totem to be whipped out to flash for us irrelevant citizens. They are scoundrels, not heroes.

Bush and Reagan even outdid Nixon in the seriousness of the offenses and the baldness of the cover-up. Nixon, after all, was only trying to subvert *parts* of the government. Reagan and Bush wanted to tear up the Constitution, then make it impossible to enforce the criminal law.

With no pressure on witnesses against them, and the still-potent magic of Reagan's "I'm just a kindly old smiling moron who didn't know what was going on," there won't be a clear picture of what happened until most of us are dead, if then. The bad guys won.

And now they plead that for the sake of national unity, we forget their crimes. Like Nixon.

The sycophants at *The Wall Street Journal* urge exactly that, that we not hound these men. They deserve hounding, for what they did and also for what they cheapened.

They even cheapened mercy.

Abraham Lincoln forgave Confederate soldiers. Warren Harding forgave the unfairly prosecuted Eugene V. Debs. Harry Truman and Jimmy Carter forgave war resisters.

These were noble acts of compassion.

Reagan and Bush pardoned George Steinbrenner and Armand Hammer, a couple of Nixon's slimy cronies.

Now Bush has reached bottom. He pardoned himself.

Observations and questions

1) The headline borrows Aregood's ending. Does this duplication undermine the kicker's punch, or does it set up the knockout punch?

2) In his first two paragraphs, Aregood names four living U.S. presidents and calls three of them "the Prince of Darkness," "a sleaze," and "dim." The average journalist might deliver one of those zingers in a whole career, if ever. If you start off that hot, do you limit or free up what you can do in the next paragraphs?

3) Sample Aregood's slangy diction, for example: "rat him out," "whacked," "crap," "smiling moron," and "slimy cronies." Does such language enhance or hurt the writer's authority with readers? How?

4) In the middle of this editorial, Aregood indirectly compares Reagan and Bush to "Saddam Hussein or George III." What images do those two names conjure up for readers?

5) Study how Aregood weaves Richard Nixon through this piece. What connotations of Nixon does he play with, and how does he control his readers' responses to them?

6) Examine the lengths and complexity of sentences in the last six paragraphs: "The sycophants . . . himself." Think about how Aregood builds a rhythm by variation, culminating in the devastating line: "He pardoned himself."

A conversation with
Richard Aregood

DON FRY: We're thinking of retiring this award, Richard, now that you've won it for the third time.

RICHARD AREGOOD: Well, why don't you give me a large amount of cash, and I'll be glad to stop entering. [Laughter]

Where do such good ideas for editorials come from?

Some from today's newspaper. Others are just ideas that germinate over a period of time. You start thinking about an issue, and after a while, your mind sorts it all out.

Do you carry a bunch of ideas around with you?

I save clippings, and stick markers in books, that sort of thing. Sometimes I have pockets full of a totally disorderly pile of clippings.

Does your staff meet to discuss ideas?

Yeah. We meet every morning. We have two writers and a man who mostly does the mechanics and layout, make-up, that sort of thing, who writes the occasional editorial. Plus an editor (me) and a cartoonist.

What do you do at those meetings?

We just get together and have our kind of a loving argument. [Laughter] And it's wonderful, because the editorials are virtually self-assigning.

[*Editor's Note: I have heavily edited and rearranged this conversation for brevity and clarity, and recomposed the questions.*]

What's the ideological stance of your paper?

In American newspaper terms, we're probably farther left than anybody, with the possible exception of the Madison *Capital Times*, the other paper that endorsed Jesse Jackson in '84. But it's not a Marxist-Leninist left; it's a kind of a 1934 CIO left.

Does your paper define itself as "not *The Philadelphia Inquirer*"?

Yeah. We certainly are not *The Inquirer*. We're a different kind of newspaper. I mean, we have no regional or national pretensions. We don't think of ourselves as anything particularly remarkable. We try to be a local newspaper, a tabloid, a big-city *Grand Forks Herald*, if that makes any sense at all.

In the Dakotas, maybe. When you're trying to be not *The Inquirer*, what do you do?

I guess we try not to do the editorials we should do, the ones that everybody thinks newspapers are obliged to do.

"Daylight Saving Time is a good idea."

Yeah. [Laughter] "It's a nice idea to give money to charity." Yes, indeed. We agree with that. And then we'll get out of it, because when you do that kind of editorial, you're almost condemning yourself not to say anything.

Do you try to be far out?

No, I think I just *am* far out. [Laughter] I try to say what I mean. I try not to be one of those editorial writers who gets tangled up with how profound things are supposed to be.

But you always seem to know what you're talking about.

Well, one of the greatest compliments I ever got was when I wrote some editorial on some arcane subject, and Gil Spencer is moaning to Zack Stalberg, "I don't know what to do. Aregood's writing about Third World trade, and it really annoys me that he actually knows this crap." [Laughter]

Indeed. And it's easier to blast away when you know what you're talking about.

We don't do what a lot of people think we do, which is walk into the saloon, pull out a gun, and start blazing away. I mean, we really do know what we're trying to do.

Do you try not to be *The Wall Street Journal*?

No. That's as far right in the Establishment as you can get. I think of us as probably opposite *The Detroit News,* which doesn't have all that ideological claptrap that those poor, right-wing children at *The Wall Street Journal* have.

Do you spread the ideological claptrap across your staff, or are you all lefties?

Well, there's a spread. I really don't know how to characterize us, because three of us are women, and two of us are black, and those differences seem to have more impact than the ideological stuff. And those differences are more interesting. They seem to have more meat on them. I'm much more a fan of ethnic diversity on editorial boards than of ideological diversity.

Has that admirable diversity changed your page?

Oh, sure. We're more feminist than other editorial pages, because on most days, there's a majority of women. And we're blacker, because two black folks are 40 percent of a small editorial board.

So people volunteer for the day's pieces.

Sometimes I make assignments. Most of the time, it becomes clear to everybody who wants to write the editorial.

After you choose what *you*'re going to write about, what's your next step?

I do something else. [Laughter] You know, I'll catch up with something, or go to lunch, or wander around and talk to people. I don't immediately turn to it and bury myself in the data, because generally speaking, I've already read the data before the meeting. So I can let my head work on it without bothering the rest of me too much.

After you wander around for a while, what happens next?

Well, then I wander around some more. [Laughter] And, once in a while, I just sit in my office.

I'm trying to picture an Aregoodian office! [Laughter]

Well, I've made my office as comfortable as possible for somebody like me. There's a collection of Lincoln and Mencken and Emerson and that sort of thing that I can use to cool myself off, and sometimes an editorial comes out of just sitting around and reading.

Then what?

Oh, about 4 o'clock, I sit down and write.

Do you have the whole thing in your head then?

I must, because I generally don't take very long to do them.

So the writing takes all day, but the typing doesn't. How do you make your editorials so clear?

Thank you. I try to say what I want to say, and I try not to clutter it up with irrelevant subject matter, or with things that will make people's eyes roll back in their heads. I just spit it the hell out.

You're just trying to reach a reader who's intelligent enough to know what you're trying to do, and your only obligation is not to get in the way.

Does the clarity come in drafting, or do you revise for clarity?

It's mostly in there. I revise for clunky transitions and that sort of thing, because I generally know where I want to go.

You know what you want to say. Do you think of your editorials in parts?

Hell, yes. I like to write essays, and an essay has a beginning, a middle, and an end. Editorials in a lot of newspapers are just 24 inches of harrumphing, and I don't have time to waste on harrumphing. It's just like the rest of the paper. If you're going to have good writing in your newspaper, you should have people telling stories, and not just spitting out data.

But essays have introductions, whereas you tend to open very fast.

Oh, I don't have time to meander. [Laughs] This is a tabloid. If I don't get people into the tent in the first five lines or so, I've lost them.

Well, your blast at Bush starts like this: "Great." One word, and we're in the tent. [Laughter]

Yeah.

Who edits you?

Generally, my deputy Don Harrison edits it.

Does he edit much, or does he just bounce it back to you for repair?

I think he smooths it. Like a lot of writers, there are words I fall in love with from time to time. And he keeps me from beating them to death.

Does he ever bounce one back to you? You are, after all, the boss, with three ASNEs and a Pulitzer....

He bounces them back and says, "I don't get it." [Laughter] At which point, I know I'm in deep.

You have a well-deserved reputation for always saying what you mean. But is there a meaner meaning kept back in your head, or do you _really_ say what you mean?

Pretty much so. When I don't say what I mean, my editorials aren't very good.

Why don't other journalists say what they mean?

Because they're trained not to. A lot of people don't have opinions. I wouldn't want anybody on my editorial board who doesn't have opinions. That's where the passion comes from. You've got to believe in something. There are a lot of things I believe in, and strongly. And you've got to care about what you're writing, or it reads like an editorial. [Laughter]

Right. Is it possible that newswriting itself wrings the passion out of journalists?

It doesn't get wrung out doing routine stories. I mean, I've covered a lot of fires and murders, and I got the addresses right, and all that sort of thing. Some of it is freedom, you know, and you hire intelligent people.

I came to this paper when I was 23 years old, in the days when Walter Annenberg owned the paper, and nobody gave a damn about it. The editors had a delightfully loose approach, and sometimes it turned out awful, and sometimes it turned out rather nicely. When you went out to cover a story, you approached it like a storyteller.

Hmmmm. So writing good stories breeds passion?

Yeah, I think so, because it's so satisfying to tell a story successfully.

Perhaps some journalists don't say what they mean because they're afraid....

Sure, and a lot don't try. You get out of school, and you go to work for a newspaper, and there's some..., some totalitarian running the place, and you..., you just start doing things his way. It never occurs to you that there's another way to do it. You may never recover from that totalitarian.

Forgive this crude transition, but let's talk about your "Bush Pardons Six" editorial. Tell me how....

I just read the story, and I got furious! I mean, that is not the American system, when you commit crimes and then forgive yourself! I think the nexus of this one is just anger, patriotic anger!

And where did the idea that Bush pardoned himself come from?

That was my first response: (EXPLETIVES DELETED TO AVOID CONFISCATION.)

He pardoned himself! Even Nixon didn't do that!

I had an idea for a column right after this atrocity happened: As soon as Bill Clinton was sworn in, his first act should have been to pardon Bush,... [Laughter]

I like that. [Laughter]

...thereby convicting him. [Laughter] Here's your lead: "Great. Now we've got the criminals forgiving themselves. Even Richard Nixon, the Prince of Darkness himself, had the good taste to find some poor boob to blow out the charges against him.

"Too chancy for a sleaze like George Bush. Or maybe he knew that Bill Clinton wasn't likely to indulge himself in self-destructive stupidity like honest but dim Jerry Ford was."

You're the only writer I know who would use the phrase: "a sleaze like George Bush." How do you get away with stuff like that?

I don't know. [Laughter] I just thought George Bush was a man who had played out his principles and honor somewhere around 1944, and ever since then had been just doing what was necessary. That's a totally personal reaction to the guy, and I'm willing to listen to other people. But I thought that he had no connection with personal honor, or any kind of principles. So it's easy for me to call him a "sleaze."

Does anybody ever call you on it when you say things like that?

Oh, yeah. [Laughs] That's part of the fun.

Do you ever get blue blasters from the upper reaches of your building?

Oh, once in a while, but usually it's second-hand, you know, "Grand Panjandrum A or B wants to know what that meant." Which is usually people's way of saying they don't like it, because the meaning was pretty clear. But I have a nice situation. People don't punish me for what I do. [Laughter].

How about calling Richard Nixon "the Prince of Darkness himself"?

Well, don't you think of Nixon as like Mephistopheles [laughs], at the center of his band of subdemons? Mephistopheles was second only to God himself, and he was the really heavy angel, and his fall was all the more tragic because of his talents, and all that sort of thing. I don't want to ruin everybody's idea of newspapermen by trying to sound literate, particularly about the Bible, but..., [Laughs], I think it fits Nixon. His fall was virtually as far as Mephistopheles's.

If only he'd stayed chained in the pit of Hell, you know, maybe we'd be all right. But he just won't cooperate; he keeps trying to crawl back.

Are you talking about Mephistopheles or Nixon? [Laughter] My first moment of political awareness came when I listened to Tricky Dick delivering the "Checkers" speech. Richard Nixon has dominated my entire political life, and still does.

That's right. I remember as a child, my mother would be ironing, and we'd watch Nixon harassing some poor accused Communist, wearing a very bad necktie. [Laughter] And I remember being frightened. Nixon and McCarthy were scary people.

You bet. In paragraph five, you say: "Forget about all the crap the Reaganisti are spreading about Iran-contra." How do you get away with using words like "crap" in a newspaper?

Prolonged employment, and many uses of words like "crap." [Laughter]

You mean you've got the editors so numbed that they let you get away with it?

That's right. [Laughs] That's something I don't think a lot of opinion writers understand, particularly young ones, that you've got to find your place. If I were writing for *The New York Times,* I wouldn't call things "crap." I might find some more literate way to say "crap." You've got to to earn your place. I don't go over the edge.

Well.... [Laughter]

Well, some days, I come mighty close to it. But after I don't know how many years I've been doing editorials, probably about 20, they know I'm not going over the edge.

I like this piece because it starts strong, and gets stronger. Listen to paragraph six: "The fact is the policy was a criminal policy, administered in secret by criminals." In paragraph nine: "He and this un-American band of conspirators...." Paragraph ten: "...and behave like some homicidal junta." The ante keeps going up, up, up, up.

Well, I think it's un-American to rape, pillage, and burn the Constitution. Sometimes, when you're writing, you just get angrier and angrier and angrier, and you just keep typing and, before long..., I mean, I've broken typewriters!

Late in the piece, you take a jab at *The Wall Street Journal,* calling them "sycophants."

Yeah, well, they sound like Elliot Abrams, talking about "the criminalization of policy differences." I mean, we're talking about actual criminal activity. And I've been writing editorials for a long time, and have, shall we say, flayed my liberal political co-religionists. But if

I were a right-winger, I'd have a lot of difficulty justifying that whole Iran-contra thing, or actually believing in it, but *The Wall Street Journal* can always find a way.

At the end, you say: "Now Bush has reached bottom. He pardoned himself." Were you tempted to lead with that?

Yeah, but then I started thinking about how ennobling the pardoning process was in the past, and particularly Warren Harding's pardoning of Debs. If ever there was a man unfairly imprisoned, it was Eugene V. Debs. And I figured I couldn't bring that concept in early enough if I put the bottom at the top. Because I think that sentence, "He pardoned himself," gains in impact if you precede it with what pardons used to mean. It just doesn't work as well without the context.

I agree, but then your headline writer stole your ending.

Yeah, I know. I hate it when that happens. [Laughs] But, what the hell, I've written headlines, and I know sometimes it's tough.

As you know, I'm a great fan of your editorials, and I think this is the best one you've written since "The British."

Ooh, thank you.

You're welcome. And I liked "The British" so much, I reprinted it in *Best Newspaper Writing 1985*. Remember?

Yeah, but this one has a more strident tone. I tried to maintain calm with "The British," but on this one, I thought ferocity was..., this sounds circumlocutious..., was..., not inappropriate. [Laughter]

How do you get your whole editorial staff to write this powerfully? And don't be afraid to take some credit here.

Well, it's no different from any other kind of teaching. I've benefited as an editor by teaching from time to time at Rutgers, or at various newspapers. So I understand the teaching role of an editor a little better.

How do you teach as an editor?

You can't just demand that people do what you want them to do. You have to turn them loose, and let them make their mistakes. Then you come in and say, "Perhaps you could have done this better if you'd done so-and-so." And generally, you have to teach people to say less.

To say less?

Yeah. To say it with stark clarity. Not to bog yourself down trying to tell everybody everything you know. Suppose you try to explain that because somebody in the Sewer Department turned a wrong switch, an entire neighborhood is buried in raw sewage.... [Laughter]

A common event in Philadelphia....

...and the short strokes are frequently what people who do something dreadful use to escape being held accountable: "Well, this happened, because that happened, because this happened, because that happened...."

So it's not their fault....

Yeah, but we're not really talking about the short strokes. The short strokes just get in the way.

Do you give your people feedback?

I try to teach. I try to let people know how we do what we do, and the rest is really up to them. I just want them to have clear opinions, clearly stated. We've established the basic line in the editorial meeting, so I don't have to worry about that anymore. And I don't care how they get there, but I want them to get there.

Can you teach punch in editorials?

Yeah. I just say, "If you have something to say, spit it out. Let people know that there are not two sides, let alone seven, on this question. There's one."

Can you teach courage?

Sure. You give them a comfortable place. Scared people have trouble being courageous. A lot of our newsrooms generate entirely too much paranoia. It's important to have editorial staffs that think of their role as almost independent. Reporters have thoughts and ideas, and it's very much worthwhile talking to them. I'm advocating a sort of a leaky wall between news and opinion. But then when you write, it's you and your pages. We are aware, by the way, [Laughs nervously] that someone can take it away from us at any moment.

Now, Richard, I want you to speak directly to editors of newspapers, and answer their question: "How can I get a hard-hitting editorial page like yours?"

You find someone with some experience, someone you believe is well enough backgrounded, independent enough, and brave enough. And you let that person take charge. And you show faith that that person will have the self-confidence to choose people with the same attributes. And if you do that, and you hire talented people, you will have an editorial page to be very proud of.

I think writing skills are imperative, and broad background. Editorial-page people should be a somewhat different sort. They should be reporters, but they should also be thinkers and analyzers.

I want an editorial-page editor who knows when you're stupefying people with data. I see a lot of editorials that just ooze research, but don't say much of anything. They say, "Here is the problem, and here are the dodecahedron sides of it." [Laughter] And there's the reader sitting there over his breakfast, and he finds a steaming dodecahedron in his lap. [Laughter]

What a ghastly image! [Laughter]

Hey, what the hell. I read editorial pages to be provoked. And the reason why I'm a little less honoring of *The New York Times* or *The Wall Street Journal* editorial pages these days is they no longer surprise me. They no longer provoke me. Still defending the indefensible. [Laughter] They're defending the gates from the Visigoths, and that's not fun.

Right. Maybe they're a little tired of modern life.

Yeah. It's more fun to be out there raising hell and swinging your broadsword. By the way, when this award was announced, I got a nice little note from the local Teamster honcho. That's another thing I would add to my list of qualifiers: people who get out in the world, who know a Teamster, who know a criminal (and I do make the distinction, by the way) [Laughter], who know all kinds of people, who can understand what's going on. The upsurge of the right has meant that we now have people who don't have the slightest idea of what ordinary people are thinking about. On that side, as well as on the left.

And how should top editors treat their new editorial-page editor?

When you get him, turn him loose. Don't drop in and say, "Could you explain to me why you called George Bush 'unprincipled?'" Leave him the hell alone.

And now, Richard, the really hard question. What if you hit so hard that people in the paper start fearing you, maybe even start disliking you?

Well, it sounds real simple, but it's incredibly difficult. You have to find a place where people want you to hit. In a lot of papers, despite protestations to the contrary, people really don't want bold columnists or tough editorial pages. You have to find a place that's comfortable with you. Look how long it took Molly Ivins to get a national reputation: 20 years after she should have. She terrified *The New York Times*. And people are not generally comfortable with boldness, so you've got to sort of sneak up on them.

The way Richard Aregood does, ha ha ha!

Chicago Tribune

Kenneth Knox

Finalist, Editorial Writing

Kenneth Knox has two degrees from the Medill School of Journalism at Northwestern University, and started his career in radio. He worked his way from sports writer in Arlington Heights, Illinois, to executive sports editor of the *Chicago Sun-Times*. Then the *Tribune* stole him away, and paced him through a series of editorships. He has written editorials since 1986.

Knox leads his readers through a Dave-Barryesque exploration of "THE INVASION OF THE GIANT AFRICAN SNAILS!" (I'm not making this up.) He shows that anything can furnish material for an editorial if you just add a little culture and wit. And kudos to whoever wrote that headline.

The dreadful cargo of escargot

APRIL 28, 1992

Snails are among those oddities of nature proving that there is some bad and good in everything. They are homely, disgusting little creatures who trace their travels with a trail of slime and whose sole purpose seems to be to munch plants and produce more snails.

But anoint them with garlic and butter, perhaps with a fine Bordeaux on the side, and their sins melt away.

Imagine a snail that can grow to 10 inches in length, reproduce prolifically and eat a banana at one sitting. Is this a nightmare, or an epicure's dream of ecstasy?

To the U.S. Department of Agriculture, it is a real-life version of one of those wonderfully bad science-fiction movies. The country, you see, may be on the verge of The Invasion of the Giant African Snails.

The tale begins at New York's Kennedy Airport, where apparently an unscrupulous pet importer smuggled in some 1,000 of these huge gastropod mollusks from Nigeria under the pretense that they were legal reptiles. (Note: It is necessary from time to time to use terms like "gastropod mollusk" to lend authority to matters of this import; it also is duly noted that some snails live only in water.) How they got past the people assigned to inspect such things is a worthy question, but what matters is what happened since.

An alert Florida agricultural inspector spotted some at a pet store in March. By the time U.S. investigators got on the trail—which probably wasn't too difficult since snails move very slowly and do leave that telltale slime—the snails had been dispersed to pet stores and home terrariums in 25 states, including Illinois.

The concern is what will happen if some get into the wild, if they haven't already. These snails devour almost any kind of fruit or vegetable, eat a fourth of their body weight in a day and can produce 1,000 offspring in a lifetime. It is not a great leap to foresee catastrophe for home gardens or commercial crops; the world is a textbook of ecological horrors from beasts transplanted to where nature didn't intend.

The department is scouring pet-store records to trace the snails and is begging for public help in rounding them up, promising amnesty for the owners. So do your part. If you own one of these monsters, or have seen one, call your local USDA office and turn it in. Or get out the garlic and butter. Lots of it.

Wayne Nicholas

Finalist, Editorial Writing

Wayne Nicholas, a 1963 graduate of the Missouri School of Journalism, has worked in six newspapers. He lists his objective as devoting himself "full-time to wholeheartedly pursuing the goal of becoming the best editorial writer in the nation." Unfortunately, he adds, his duties as managing editor get in the way.

Since you probably don't live in Cleveland, Mississippi, you have to read this editorial as what it is, a fable. Nicholas shows how the best intentions turn into lip service for our schools. If we keep cooking the golden geese, our children won't even understand the fables about them.

WONDERLAND
There once was a great goose...

FEBRUARY 11, 1992

In the Kingdom of Wonderland there once lived a great white goose, named Schooling, which we are told was capable of laying golden eggs.

Everybody had high hopes for Schooling, because they knew if she were treated right she would empower the children of Wonderland to hold their own in a world which was constantly becoming more and more complicated and competitive. They also knew that if Schooling were in good shape she could help Wonderland feather all its nests because badly needed factories wouldn't hesitate to flock to Wonderland if their owners knew their children, too, could benefit from such a magnificent goose.

At first Wonderland was run by a King, named Maybe, who loved Schooling and wanted to be known as Schooling's best friend. There was only one thing he wouldn't do for Schooling—he wouldn't go to his subjects and ask them to pay enough taxes so that Schooling could have the kind of food she needed to lay the golden eggs.

The people in Wonderland's parliament felt pretty much the same way. They even adopted a lengthy document, titled "Schooling Reform," which they said would guarantee Schooling would produce golden eggs, but there was just one thing they wouldn't do. They wouldn't let any of the people in the land take a chance in a lottery to raise money to buy the food Schooling needed to produce those golden eggs.

Many of Wonderland's subjects were miffed by these objections, because they loved Schooling, and since they were farmers they understood they were already taking a gamble anyway—every time they planted a seed in the ground.

Well, this went on for four long years, and Schooling became quite gaunt and her appearance was, at best, bedraggled. Eventually, Schooling stopped laying eggs altogether, and day after day, her waddle became slower and slower. Finally, one day Schooling scrunched down in her nest and just kind of stuck her head under her wings and shut her eyes.

Shortly after that a new king, named Misfortune, ascended to the throne. He thought too much emphasis had been placed on Schooling, and that the coop Schooling was living in was taking too much from the royal treasury, even though it was quite run down by that time. He wasted little love on Schooling or the people, themselves, who said they loved Schooling. He told them "to get real." The money wasn't there to buy the food Schooling needed.

Finally one day he took a good look at Schooling and saw how ungainly she had become. Initially, he grabbed her by the neck and dragged her through the mud and mire, claiming that Schooling's keepers had ruined her by spending much of the money that was intended for her food on the coop's administration.

Then someone told him how long it had been since Schooling had produced a single golden egg for Wonderland. In a fit of ire, Misfortune ordered Schooling cooked.

After that, the predictable happened. The children of Wonderland all faltered and were unable to make their own in the world. Never again did a business firm ever consider moving to Wonderland.

We understand the people of Wonderland were pretty fed up when they finally awoke and found out what had happened to Schooling, and we are told that in cooking the goose that laid the golden eggs, King Misfortune cooked his own goose as well.

Observations on editorial writing

A lot of people, especially in the newspaper business, make a mistake about what an editorial should be. They think its only purpose is to state an opinion. That's like saying the purpose of a poem is to convey information.

An editorial can do many things. In fact, it can do almost anything. What distinguishes it from other forms of journalism are its freedom from the discipline of neutrality and its subjection to the discipline of brevity. It ought to work like a sonnet rather than an epic.

The best editorials tell you much more than what to believe or how to vote. They tell you about the community the newspaper serves, its distinctive language and intellectual style, its enthusiasms and indispositions, its wildest hopes. They also tell you about the newspaper. Every editorial talks about itself, even if it scrupulously avoids the first person plural. Turn to an editorial page of a newspaper, and you will find out quickly whether the newspaper is bold or timorous, subtle or reductive, intellectually honest or captious, graceful or deadly earnest. You will also find out what the newspaper as a whole thinks about writing.

In this year's ASNE contest for editorial writing, a satisfyingly large number of papers seemed to think quite well of it. The tone of the top entries ranged from the blunt, side-of-the-mouth approach of three-time winner Richard Aregood of the *Philadelphia Daily News* to the allegorical imagination of Wayne Nicholas's runner-up pieces from the Cleveland (Miss.) *Bolivar Commercial,* and the bemused grace of runner-up Ken Knox from my paper, the *Chicago Tribune.* All of these and many others that did not win had style, rigor, and eloquence. It is a pleasure to honor the best of them now.

Jack Fuller, Editor
Chicago Tribune

Charles Klaveness
Headline Writing

CHARLES KLAVENESS, 49, of *The New York Times* is the first copy editor to win the ASNE Distinguished Writing Award. He's also the first copy editor ever eligible for the award, in this year's Headline Writing category.

Klaveness was born February 14, 1944, in New Orleans, Louisiana. He is married to Jan O'Donnell Klaveness, a fiction writer. He received his B.A. in English from Tulane University in 1966, and Columbia University granted him the M.S. in journalism in 1973. He joined *The New York Times* in 1979.

Charles Klaveness makes good writers look good. His witty, literate writing propels readers straight to the lead.

Congratulations to you, Charles, and to all copy editors.

Clocks are fugitive: Will Father Time now carry a watch?

JANUARY 1, 1992

By Betsy Wade

Last night, anyone with a television set and the stamina to fight off sleep could watch 1991 count itself out of existence. But other than those expiring nanoseconds, the passing of the year was hard to track, because clocks are fading from neighborhood walls, and time's component minutes and hours plop into oblivion unheralded.

Not to say there aren't fancy new clocks: for one, those micronumbers on the VCR, although the time is often wrong because of lapses in resetting the displays. But those numbers with a blinking hiatal colon serve only the insomniac, giving unwanted news, namely that anxiety has consumed one-quarter of a night's sleep, and still counting.

And in the large department, Aiwa has put up a digital display at 47th Street overlooking Times Square that is excellent for monitoring the speed of the TKTS line, an experience that has something in common with insomnia. And there is the new macro news board between 45th and 46th Streets, which occasionally displays mammoth numbers, courtesy of Metropolitan Life, which may have a vested interest in keeping everyone upright and moving. But neither of these can be read by people leaving the subway at 42d Street, who are the ones who need to know whether they are late to work or, Lord forbid, the dentist.

For them, the real loss is the eye-level clocks, those old friends that told how well the rat race was being run. A case in point is the huge advertising clock that once stood beside the Riverside Drive viaduct at 125th Street. As the downtown IRT left the tunnel under Broadway

Must Father Time Now Carry a Watch?

Continued From Page 25

motionless and the dentist calls the next patient you can look all up and down the subway car in vain, not finding one eavesdroppable wristwatch.

I had a friend who settled in New York from Madison, Wis., a Midwest capital with a skyline and other pretensions. She returned to La Guardia Airport one afternoon after a visit some years ago and seemed to inhale the scurry as a baby fills its lungs. "Home again!" she said. "Madison is really too slow for me now." What restored the spring to her step? New Yorkers hurrying past clocks, circular and digital, dancing their galliard to the silent song of those pacemakers.

New Yorkers need clocks as rowers on a trireme need a drumbeat. Grand Central Terminal knows this, and Bulova, too, which rounds up the Penn Station remuda with a digital display at Seventh Avenue and 34th Street. But where are the shop clocks, the ones that gave cadence to north-south ebbs and flows?

In former times, if you hoofed along running errands — chocolate Santas or candy corn at Mondel's, a gift at Shakespeare & Company, a gaudy windbreaker (Size 6X) at Morris Brothers, a replacement "Ferdinand" at Eeyore's — you could glance into the glass windows of the shoe-repair shops and glom the illuminated Cat's Paw clocks on the back wall and know if the day's duties should be taken motto presto or lento. If you did it downtown, there was always one embedded in the sidewalk in front of the jeweler William Barthman, which has been at Broadway and Maiden Lane "since 1884."

Knowing the time did not really involve reading the clock; the process involved neurons, the devices that flick your finger back from the stove before your brain says "hot." The posture of the clock hands told your feet to pick up the pace, or saunter, without intervention of the brain.

Barber shops used to have clocks up on their white walls. Now barber shops have been spliced into unisex

Scurriers need big and little hands in plain view.

beauty salons called Shear Delight or Clip Joint or A Cut Above and clocks are apparently déclassé. This is not the case, I hasten to add, with my hair salon, because I will not of my own free will permit myself to be wound in a sheet in any place where I cannot know the time. To give my atelier its due, Christopher has a name with no pun, as well as a gigantic clock on the wall adjusted for Dora Alba's seat so I can read the time forward in the mirror because there is a mirror on the facing wall, too.

The surviving old-timey barber shops have become clockless; whoever distributed to barbers has gone the way of Cat's Paw. That is, when the old clocks wore out, Ed Pinaud's or Zotos or whosoever's bay rum did not hustle in a replacement.

Bars still need clocks, even if five minutes fast, and the brewers are still in the business of supplying them. But these have never been part of it: pressing one's nose to a saloon glass is not cool; it is embarrassing and uses almost as much time as taking out your watch.

In fact, New Yorkers do not really look at clocks: they feel them as tide feels the moon, as the monarch butterfly senses the declining light. If Mayor Dinkins fears that things are slowing, he might want to float Big Tock Bonds, to restore our cadence, our distinctive pace. Give every tiny Lotto-cigarette stall tucked in front of every store a legible clock. Give the rolling side of New Yorkers a way to measure their days once more.

Fred R. Conrad/The New York Times
Aiwa's digital display clock at 47th Street and Broadway.

to bridge the Harlem Valley, you could gaze toward the river and know your E.T.A. at work or, Lord forbid, the dentist. That big face went away when they rebuilt the viaduct and, while a billboard is again in place, there's an information gap out there.

I shrink from an obsessive topic, but subway clocks are on the agenda. The lords of transit took the big classical oak-cased clocks, operated by storage batteries, out of the subway stations 20-odd years ago. Some genius decided that the city should not pay to operate and repair clocks to inform the riders, but that advertisers should pay the city to sell their merchandise, with the lure an adjoining clock. So it was that cigarette makers began to flog their wares from illuminated clocks in the subway, where, unbeknownst to above-ground moguls, smoking is illegal.

The rub in this capitalist tool is that clocks hang in stations where advertisers think customers are, but not on a need-to-know basis. How long have you waited on the platform for the No. 1 or 9 at 96th Street? No clock there will tell you. Change at 72d Street? No way to know if you are that pressed. At 116th Street, Columbia students get a platform clock, which perhaps compensates for the loss of the lollipop model outside the defunct Prexy's. But City College's students at 137th, every bit as deserving and with a rugged hill to climb, have no way of knowing if the gong has sounded.

Since privatization is the watchword, people are now expected to turn to each other. But the portal to privately maintained timepieces closed with the advent of the digital watch. As the train sits motionless and the dentist calls the next patient you can look all up and down the subway car in vain, not finding one eavesdroppable wristwatch.

I had a friend who settled in New York from Madison, Wis., a Midwest capital with a skyline and other pretensions. She returned to La Guardia Airport one afternoon after a visit some years ago and seemed to inhale the scurry as a baby fills its lungs. "Home again!" she said. "Madison is really too slow for me now." What restored the spring to her step? New Yorkers hurrying past clocks, circular and digital, dancing their galliard to the silent song of those pacemakers.

New Yorkers need clocks as rowers on a trireme need a drumbeat. Grand Central Terminal knows this, and Bulova, too, which rounds up the Penn Station remuda with a digital display at Seventh Avenue and 34th Street. But where are the shop clocks, the ones that gave cadence to north-south ebbs and flows?

In former times, if you hoofed along running errands—chocolate Santas or candy corn at Mondel's, a gift at Shakespeare & Company, a gaudy windbreaker (Size 6X) at Morris Brothers, a replacement "Ferdinand" at Eeyore's—you could glance into the glass windows of the shoe-repair shops and glom the illuminated Cat's Paw clocks on the back wall and know if the day's duties should be taken molto presto or lento. If you did it downtown, there was always one embedded in the sidewalk in front of the jeweler William Barthman, which has been at Broadway and Maiden Lane "since 1884."

Knowing the time did not really involve reading the clock; the process involved neurons, the devices that flick your finger back from the stove before your brain says "hot." The posture of the clock hands told your feet to pick up the pace, or saunter, without intervention of the brain.

Barber shops used to have clocks up on their white walls. Now barber shops have been spliced into unisex beauty salons called Shear Delight or Clip Joint or A Cut Above and clocks are apparently déclassé. This is not the case, I hasten to add, with my hair salon, because I will not of my own free will permit myself to be wound in a sheet in any place where I cannot know the time. To give my atelier its due, Christopher has a name with no pun, as well as a gigantic clock on the wall adjusted for Dora Alba's seat so I can read the time forward in the mirror because there is a mirror on the facing wall, too.

The surviving old-timey barber shops have become clockless; whoever distributed to barbers has gone the way of Cat's Paw. That is, when the old clocks wore out, Ed Pinaud's or Zotos or whosoever's bay rum did not hustle in a replacement.

Bars still need clocks, even if five minutes fast, and the brewers are still in the business of supplying them. But these have never been part of it: pressing one's nose to a saloon glass is not cool; it is embarrassing and uses almost as much time as taking out your watch.

In fact, New Yorkers do not really *look* at clocks: they feel them as tide feels the moon, as the monarch butterfly senses the declining light. If Mayor Dinkins fears that things are slowing, he might want to float Big Tock Bonds, to restore our cadence, our distinctive pace. Give every tiny Lotto-cigarette stall

tucked in front of every store a legible clock.
Give the rolling tide of New Yorkers a way to
measure their days once more.

Observations and questions

1) Should headlines always tell what the story is about? This one doesn't.

2) The image of Father Time appears nowhere in this story, but notice the date: January 1. How much latitude can the copy editor take in bringing in elements from outside the story?

3) The word "fugitive" puns on the Latin *tempus fugit* (Time flies). Puns can have many levels, depending on the mutual knowledge of the copy editor and various readers. But we should never require our readers to understand the pun in order to understand the headline. Journalistic art is people art.

4) Write a headline for this story exclusively from the lead paragraph without duplicating any of its words. Hard, isn't it? Now write one exclusively from the final paragraph, again with no duplication. Harder.

5) Klaveness modifies his headline in the jumpline: "Must Father Time Now Carry a Watch?" Compose a series of jumplines for this story, based on the words in the headline. Remember that many readers initially enter the story through the jumpline.

Currents | Dulcie Leimbach

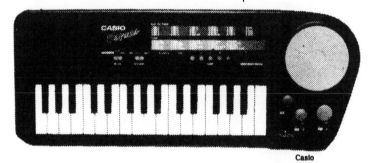

Casio

Wanna Rap? Let It Rip: All You Do Is Add the Lip

EVER since rap music began its segue from being public enemy No. 1 to being an uneasy buddy of the mainstream, it has been only a matter of time until a rap keyboard would wend its way into the crib.

(Crib: that's house, for the uninitiated.)

Listen up: Casio's new Rapman does just about everything a bona fide rap group does.

The keyboard has 25 instrument sounds (including piano, metal guitar, brass ensemble, electric bass); several sound effects (like a car horn and a siren); 30 background rhythms that genuine rap music cannot live without (such as "funky," "rhythm and blues" and "hip hop"); a distorter that can change a voice from low pitch to high, and even a scratch disk for simulating the warped sound that skids through just about every rap song on the charts.

Rapman has only one built-in microphone for those who want to do a little frontin' (showing off), but that's O.K. A little sharing never hurt.

The portable keyboard, which runs on batteries, is 20¼ inches long and weighs about three pounds. It sells for about $99 at many Wiz, Toys "R" Us and K Mart stores. The stores haven't restocked Rapman since Christmas, but their representatives said that more deliveries were imminent.

Observations and questions

1) This head scans; speak it out.
   You can count,   without a doubt.
   On strong words, put a beat.
   Sound it out,   tap your feet.
   Forget the "is"; it's a snap.
   Anything   scans in rap.

2) See if you can scan the headline on this story. Put accents on the strong syllables and see what you get. Substitute a colon for "is," and it's perfect. Readers don't read headlines aloud, but they may perceive meter.

3) These headline words appear in the story: "it, rap, do, is, the." These do not: "wanna, let, rip, all, you, add, lip." In short, only one key word appears in the headline. What other words in the story could help make a headline?

4) This headline is a copy editor's dream: All the words are short. Unfortunately, short words, especially lots of them, can make a headline sound simple-minded, even folksy.

We Are the World;
We Are the Crayons

TEACHERS and children from the Montgomery County school district in Maryland, just north of Washington, were tired of seeing the Rev. Dr. Martin Luther King Jr. being drawn with a black crayon. The problem was Crayola packed its flesh-colored crayons (hues from apricot to mahogany) only in its 64-pack, which was too big for the pupils' small hands.

Heeding the call for a new age of multiculturalism (and marketing), Binney & Smith, the Easton, Pa., company that makes Crayolas, slipped the existing skin-tone crayons into their own box.

"Teachers wanted children to color drawings of themselves to reflect how they think they look," said Mark O'Brien, a spokesman for the company.

The new eight-crayon box carries apricot, peach, tan, sepia, burnt sienna and mahogany, plus black and white. And it has a new logo: a colorfully correct green and blue globe ringed with the words "multicultural colors." This "global pack" is available only through Chaselle, a Columbia, Md., school-supplies distributor, at (800) 242-7355.

Binney & Smith is awaiting feedback from schools and teachers before it decides whether to sell the set retail.

Observations and questions

1) Substitute "Crayolas" for "Crayons" in this headline. Why doesn't it sound right?

2) Readers have to know the song "We Are the World..." to understand this headline, and probably every hearing person in the western world does. Readers swim in a world rich with such popular cultural icons, and copy editors can draw on them. But how can we judge whether enough readers will recognize such an allusion? What percentage is enough?

3) Try writing a headline on this story with the word "multicultural" in it.

4) Try writing a headline on this story using the colors mentioned in the fourth paragraph.

English bathrooms: Out of the closet

JANUARY 23, 1992

By William E. Schmidt

LONDON, Jan. 22—The term water closet may sound like a quaint euphemism, but over the years it has also come to be a pretty fair description of the typical British bathroom. As often as not, it is a cramped, airless cubicle, a kind of architectural afterthought crouched at the end of a creaky hallway or hidden beneath the stairs of a 19th-century terrace house.

But in the last few years, the British bathroom has begun to come into its own. Not only are new houses equipped with larger and more luxurious bathrooms, but there is a growing trend to remodel and update old bathrooms, often using florid antique or reproduction fixtures that evoke the look and feel of Victorian manor houses.

And there has been a sudden explosion in the consumer market for showers and shower stalls, to either replace or supplement that most essential British fixture, the bathtub. The most elaborate are advertised as "power showers" because they employ hydraulic pumps, often noisy, to augment the chronically weak household water pressure. Built directly into bathroom walls, they cost $200 to $1,000, depending on spray options and flow rate.

"For years, Britons wouldn't hear of showers, partly because they liked their baths, and partly because we just don't have the proper water pressure like you do in America," said Stephen Quigley, the managing director of Richmond's, a large plumbing supply store in southwest London. In most English houses, water pressure is dependent on a gravity-fed tank in a loft or an attic.

"But I think the bath is going the way of the full breakfast," Mr. Quigley added. "It's a life style thing. People don't have time in the morning for a leisurely bath or breakfast."

In pushing out their bathroom walls and abandoning bathtubs for shower stalls, Britons may be doing something much more substantial than flirting with the latest trend in interior design. They are, in a way, tinkering with their own cultural plumbing, a trend that some consider vaguely unsettling.

What was once a euphemism is now a fancy.

"Perhaps there is a bit of snobbery about it, but I think the idea that a bathroom ought to be carpeted and wallpapered and painted in peach colors is absurd, even vulgar," said Gavin Stamp, an architect, writer and member of the Victorian Society, which works to preserve and celebrate 19th-century architecture. "Bathrooms do matter. But they ought to be well plumbed and solid: substantial, like the engine room of a ship."

Indeed, some essential breakthroughs in sanitary engineering and indoor plumbing took place in 19th-century Britain as a result of the work of Thomas Crapper, who invented the siphonless flushing mechanism, and the Rev. Edward Johns, who introduced his popular "dolphin" toilet to the United States at the Philadelphia Centennial Exposition of 1876.

Moreover, some 19th-century English fixtures were extraordinarily ornate, a reflection of the Victorian love of machinery: enameled hand basins and fluted toilet bowls and gold and brass taps and fixtures. Some public restrooms were adventures in sanitary wonderland.

For example, in one tank in central London in the late 19th century, the flushing water was held in a suspended glass globe in which an attendant kept goldfish. (The mechanics of the device assured that the goldfish would not be lost in the flush.)

Indoor toilets were not uncommon in British houses by the late 19th century, but the emphasis on bathing as a matter of general hygiene was much slower to catch on. Min Hogg, editor in chief of *The World of Interiors,* the magazine that perhaps best captures the eccentricity of British decorating, said the English seemed to develop a sense of the bathroom that differed from what was evolving on the Continent and across the Atlantic. "That's why the French have the bidet, and we do not, and the Americans have showers, and we do not," Ms. Hogg said.

Bathrooms were not common in working-class housing projects until after World War I, said John Pennell, the director of the British Bathroom Council, an organization that represents big manufacturers of bathroom products. Even then, they tended to be very cramped; they were quite deliberately made the absolute minimum size. Their design, he said, probably reflected some degree of class bias.

"I think most architects, who were middle class, had a difficult time being persuaded that bathrooms were really necessary for working-class people," Mr. Pennell said.

Over the years, the relatively spare, compact British bathroom has attracted the curiosity of foreigners. They have marveled at the absence of a bidet or shower, at the fact that the toilet is often sequestered in a tiny room all its own, and at the plumbing of sinks, which invariably have separate taps for dispensing hot and cold water. Beppe Severgnini, an Italian journalist who wrote *Inglisi,* a social history of the English published last year by Hodder & Stoughton, said this meant that washing one's hands in England required choosing "between getting your hands scorched under the hot tap or frozen under the cold one."

Mr. Severgnini concluded that the British have what he called a "troubled relationship" with their bathrooms, underscoring the point by noting that the English commonly use more than a dozen euphemisms to describe a bathroom. Among them are loo, gents', ladies', lavatory, toilet, convenience, lav, water closet, W.C., bog, john, can, head, latrine, privy and powder room.

But Mr. Pennell and others argue that the British are changing. Although the recession has slowed conversions and remodeling, the British Bathroom Council estimates that nearly half of all British houses now have showers, as against only about 30 percent a decade ago.

One house with a "power shower" is that of David Deane, a London businessman, and his wife, Karen.

"The old bathtub, with its hand-held shower, was fine if you had an hour to spare," said Mr. Deane, adding that he fell in love with brisk morning showers on trips to the United States and had a shower installed in his house in 1987. "The problem was, the dribble of water you got was never enough to get the soap off. I used to keep a pitcher beside the tub, to fill up and bang over my head, to rinse off properly."

As Mr. Pennell sees it, "The idea now is that the bathroom is part of the living space and ought to reflect the way people see themselves."

To that end, for example, Armitage Shanks, the largest British maker of bathroom equipment, now markets complete bathroom suites in a variety of styles and colors with names like oyster, chablis, peach and champagne. One suite, the Clivenden, is designed along Edwardian lines; it has fluted basins and a mahogany toilet seat.

There is also a big market for antique bathroom fixtures salvaged from junkyards and demolition projects. In the last two years, at least half a dozen shops offering reconditioned basins, taps and heavy fixtures, like re-enameled cast-iron tubs with claw-and-ball feet and rolled edges, have opened in London.

Because the fittings are not the same size as modern pipes, they are often difficult to install, and much heavier than modern appliances, a hazard in itself. A man who put a reconditioned antique marble tub into his Belgravia row house not long ago returned home to discover it in the basement, where it had halted after crashing through three floors on its way down from a loft bathroom.

Observations and questions

1) The phrase "out of the closet" has connotations of homosexuals, which has nothing to do with this story. How can we avoid distracting readers with unintended connotations?

2) Klaveness plays with "water closet" from the lead in his headline. Readers who don't know this British term may have to read the top of the story to understand the headline.

3) Substitute "British" for "English" in this headline. What effects does the alliteration cause?

4) Klaveness wrote the pullout: "What was once a euphemism is now a fancy." Think of all the meanings you can come up with for "fancy." How many of them operate in this story?

Lots of pomp, and a little happenstance

MAY 27, 1992

By Betsy Wade

Every year in the academic season, a riddle has haunted me: Earning a degree never wins you the right to wear the fancy clothes that go with it. Think about it. When you stand up to seize a bachelor's diploma, you wear a gown and hat, but no hood because the right to wear it has not yet been conferred. If you chase the sheepskin further, you get to wear the bachelor's hood from last time out, a molting sort of plumage, but not the full peacock colors you are receiving that day. And so forth.

The only way to don your just deserts is to find a still later occasion to suit up. The obvious later occasions are bootless, because no college invites you to strut with the degree candidates merely because you have financed a child's education. The college to which you have dispatched many checks simply invites you to stand by in mufti and try not to dampen your child's robe in joy.

Egad, why earn a degree if you never get to flaunt it? To solve this, and to see how I looked in a master's hood for journalism, a lowish discipline so strongly associated with yellow that the velvet hood band is that very color, I did the unforgivable. I asked. A letter went to my alma mater, Barnard, inquiring if possibly an occasion might arise when the president would be unable to attend some dismal, neglected, remote investiture, and that I might be designated to stand and march in her place. Desperate, I threw in my last bargaining point: I'd pay the air fare.

My college has sangfroid. Last winter, I got a letter asking if I would like to march in lieu of the president, Ellen Futter, not at East Cupcake Normal, but in the big leagues, at the May 1

inauguration of the new president of Marymount Manhattan College in New York. The
college said it would rent plumage for me if I
would reply with my head size and other material facts. I filled in the blanks and told the
president's office I stood ready for this service
to alma mater.

In March, a box about the size of a Pizza
Hut offering was delivered, containing a wrinkly black gown, a droopy yellow-bound hood
with a gaudy blue and white satin lining, and a
mortar board, Size 7⅜.

To get the hang of the headgear, I took to
wearing it around the house. The tassel was
fun: it can be flapped the way fifth graders
fling their braids with an emphatic "No." The
letter carrier was taken aback one day, but in
the process I learned to bend without having
the cap slide off.

Then I tried on the whole get-up, and declared war against the wrinkles. My academic
peers, ahem, know that master's gowns are not
easy to iron, because they have bassetlike flaps
like those on Edith Sitwell's headdress, but
depending vestigially from the sleeves. When
you go to steam the upper sleeve, the flaps slip
off the board and drop to the floor, dragging
in the dust. This annoyance is probably created to make one covetous of earning a doctoral gown with those wide striped sleeves.
Ironing was followed by brushing, then hanging up on the outside of a door, just for gazing. I turned it weekly so it would not fade on
one side.

I became a pest to the dean's office at Marymount, calling weekly to learn where I was to
get into my regalia. In a way I hoped I would
have to arrive in my outfit, unfurling academically from a cab, perhaps. Marymount was
slightly puzzled about robing, too, because its
president, Regina S. Peruggi, was to be inaugurated at the Madison Avenue Presbyterian
Church, not exactly on the regular jogging trail
for a college set up by the Religious of the Sacred Heart of Mary.

Lots of Pomp, and a Little Happenstance

By BETSY WADE

EVERY year in the academic season, a riddle has haunted me: Earning a degree never wins you the right to wear the fancy clothes that go with it. Think about it. When you stand up to seize a bachelor's diploma, you wear a gown and hat, but no hood because the right to wear it has not yet been conferred. If you chase the sheepskin further, you get to wear the bachelor's hood from last time out, a molting sort of plumage, but not the full peacock colors you are receiving that day. And so forth.

The only way to don your just deserts is to find a still later occasion to suit up. The obvious later occasions are bootless, because no college invites you to strut with the degree candidates merely because you have financed a child's education. The college to which you have dispatched many checks simply invites you to stand by in mufti and try not to dampen your child's robe in joy.

Egad, why earn a degree if you never get to flaunt it? To solve this, and to see how I looked in a master's hood for journalism, a lowish discipline so strongly associated with yellow that the velvet hood band in that very color, I did the unforgivable. I

asked. A letter went to my alma mater, Barnard, inquiring if possibly an occasion might arise when the president would be unable to attend some dismal, neglected, remote investiture, and that I might be designated to stand and march in her place. Desperate, I threw in my last bargaining point: I'd pay the air fare.

My college has sangfroid. Last winter, I got a letter asking if I would like to march in lieu of the president, Ellen Futter, not at East Cupcake Normal, but in the big leagues, at the May 1 inauguration of the new president of Marymount Manhattan College in New York. The college said it would rent plumage for me if I would reply with my head size and other material facts. I filled in the blanks and told the president's office I stood ready for this service to alma mater. In March, a box about the size of a Pizza Hut offering was delivered, containing a wrinkly black gown, a droopy yellow-bound hood with a gaudy blue and white satin lining, and a mortar board, Size 7¾.

To get the hang of the headgear, I took to wearing it around the house. The tassel was fun: it can be flapped the way fifth graders fling their braids with an emphatic "No." The letter carrier was taken aback one day, but in the process I learned to bend without having the cap slide off.

Then I tried on the whole get-up, and declared war against the wrinkles. My academic peers, ahem, know that master's gowns are not easy to iron, because they have bassetlike flaps like those on Edith Sitwell's headdress but depending vestigially from the sleeves. When you go to steam the upper sleeve, the flaps slip off the board and drop to the floor, dragging in the dust. This annoyance is probably created to make one covetous of earning a doctoral gown with those wide striped sleeves. Ironing was followed by brushing, then hanging up on the outside of a door, just for gazing. I turned it weekly so it would not fade on one side.

I became a pest to the dean's office

The long trail to the right tassle.

at Marymount, calling weekly to learn where I was to get into my regalia. In a way I hoped I would have to arrive in my outfit, unfurling academically from a cab, perhaps. Marymount was slightly puzzled about robing, too, because its president, Regina S. Peruggi, was to be inaugurated at the Madison Avenue Presbyterian Church, not exactly on the regular jogging trail for a college set up by the Religious of the Sacred Heart of Mary.

Well, robing was in the church basement, and little sandwiches and coffee were dished up for the inheritors of the academic procession.

Just as I had dreamed, the church basement was an academic rainbow. My black looked dowdy next to the University of Connecticut's royal turquoise, so I moved away from him. I spotted a well-turned-out fellow Columbian, a younger woman, and fluttered over to learn what part of our mutual university she was representing. "I'm Regina Peruggi," she said. "I'm being inaugurated today." I blushed to the tip of my tassel, but managed to remember my marching orders. "President Futter and Barnard College extend their congratulations, Dr. Peruggi," I said, sticking out a hand entangled in a sleeve flap. She thanked me.

It took me a couple of minutes longer to sort out why the Marymount president bore Columbia Teachers College colors, and then I realized

that working academics also wear the insignia of their alma maters, rather than that of their employers.

While I was trying to retract my purse into my sleeve flap, we were called to marching order, according to the year of the founding of our schools. Newest schools first. La Guardia (1971) sent its president, Raymond C. Bowen. Yale (1701), miles to the rear, sent an alumnus. At 100-plus, Barnard earned me a nice placement in the line. Then a really young woman asked what era I represented. "Barnard, 1889," I said. Sliding in beside me, she said: "That's where I belong. I'm Kelly Gallagher, Converse College, '88. Converse was also founded in 1889."

I sounded like Liza Minnelli singing "Ring Them Bells."

"Converse?" I squeaked. "Converse College in Spartanburg, S.C.? That's where my grandmother taught. Greek and history, until she married my grandfather." Ms. Gallagher, a senior at Union Theological, said it was the very same, and we discussed spring at Columbia and spring in the South.

It was a splendid inauguration. Regina Peruggi Day was proclaimed in Manhattan, and the Governor and Mayor sent greetings. Mrs. Eugene M. Lang, class of 1999, who is in her 70's and is the oldest undergraduate, greeted Dr. Peruggi for the students, speaking of the "golden school days" for which she had waited so long. Then, when Dr. Peruggi talked about the ties of family and academia, my heart left the church and Madison Avenue entirely.

If the Collegiate Cap and Gown Company Division of Herff Jones Inc., which sent me complete instructions about what to do in the event of rain, wants to know, it was not rain that spotted the front of the gown I duly returned to them. It was me, joining an academic procession too long for any building of mortar, marching in the 1889 rank with my tall, terrifying grandmother, carrying her — our — Shakespeare books.

Peter de Sève

Well, robing was in the church basement, and little sandwiches and coffee were dished up for the inheritors of the academic procession.

Just as I had dreamed, the church basement was an academic rainbow. My black looked dowdy next to the University of Connecticut's royal turquoise, so I moved away from him. I spotted a well-turned-out fellow Columbian, a younger woman, and fluttered over to learn what part of our mutual university she was representing. "I'm Regina Peruggi," she said. "I'm being inaugurated today." I blushed to the tip of my tassel, but managed to remember my marching orders. "President Futter and Barnard College extend their congratulations, Dr. Peruggi," I said, sticking out a hand entangled in a sleeve flap. She thanked me.

It took me a couple of minutes longer to sort out why the Marymount president bore Columbia Teachers College colors, and then I realized that working academics also wear the insignia of their alma maters, rather than that of their employers.

While I was trying to retract my purse into my sleeve flap, we were called to marching order, according to the year of the founding of our schools. Newest schools first. La Guardia (1971) sent its president, Raymond C. Bowen. Yale (1701), miles to the rear, sent an alumnus. At 100-plus, Barnard earned me a nice placement in the line. Then a really young woman asked what era I represented. "Barnard, 1889," I said. Sliding in beside me, she said: "That's where I belong. I'm Kelly Gallagher, Converse College, '88. Converse was also founded in 1889."

I sounded like Liza Minnelli singing "Ring Them Bells."

"Converse?" I squeaked. "Converse College in Spartanburg, S.C.? That's where my grandmother taught. Greek and history, until she married my grandfather." Ms. Gallagher, a senior at Union Theological, said it was the very same, and we discussed spring at Columbia and spring in the South.

It was a splendid inauguration. Regina Peruggi Day was proclaimed in Manhattan, and the Governor and Mayor sent greetings. Mrs. Eugene M. Lang, class of 1999, who is in her 70's and is the oldest undergraduate, greeted Dr. Peruggi for the students, speaking of the "golden school days" for which she had waited so long. Then, when Dr. Peruggi talked about the ties of family and academia, my heart left the church and Madison Avenue entirely.

If the Collegiate Cap and Gown Company Division of Herff Jones Inc., which sent me complex instructions about what to do in the event of rain, wants to know, it was not rain that spotted the front of the gown I duly returned to them. It was me, joining an academic procession too long for any building of mortar, marching in the 1889 rank with my tall, terrifying grandmother, carrying her—our—Shakespeare books.

Observations and questions

1) This headline plays on "Pomp and Circumstance," the march usually played for graduation processionals. What happens in the readers' heads when they get to "*happen*stance?"

2) None of the major words of this headline appear in the story. Would you prefer no words duplicated, or some, or all? Why?

3) Search this story for likely headline words and concepts. The writer uses a wide vocabulary with lots of wordplay, a copy editor's dream. That's why the best writers get the best headlines. What are you doing to get the best headlines on your stories?

4) The second paragraph begins like this: "The only way to don your just deserts is to find a still later occasion to suit up." Create a headline out of "don your just deserts." Have you helped the author or stolen the punch of a neat turn of phrase?

5) Klaveness got a lot of grief for a pullout he wrote for this story: "The long trail to the right tassle." Yes, "tass*le*" is misspelled here, although correct in the sixth paragraph of the story. Copy editors need copyediting too.

A conversation with
Charles Klaveness

DON FRY: You're the first copy editor to win this writing prize. Actually, you're the first copy editor ever *eligible* for it. So, congratulations.

CHARLES KLAVENESS: Thank you. Almost every year, the Pulitzer Prizes are announced, and we copy editors participate in the glory. We're glad to have had a part in it. We congratulate those to whom the prizes go, but then we put our heads down and go back to work. It's a real high for all copy editors to know that we can be singled out too. Thanks very much from all of us.

You're welcome. And on behalf of all writers, I'd like to thank all copy editors everywhere for saving our necks every day.
 Somehow, copy editors seem contradictory: you "put your heads down" and get everything right, but you've just won this prize by writing *playful* headlines.

I wasn't always a playful headline writer. When I walked in the door of The Good Gray Lady here, I was fully intimidated. I wrote a couple of snappy headlines and somebody noticed, in particular, the man who was then news editor, who's now an assistant managing editor, by the name of Allan Siegal. I'll spell his name for you.

Mr. Siegal would want you to get it right.

Yes, indeed, he would. That's why I'm looking it up. [Laughter]

[Editor's Note: I have heavily edited and rearranged this conversation for brevity and clarity, recomposed the questions, and copyedited everything.]

He's probably the most famous copy editor in America.

That's why I'm looking it up. [Laughter] A-L-L-A-N M-period S-I-E-G-A-L.

A name with lots of traps in it. So he encouraged you?

He encouraged me in the same way the other editors did. I can't remember that he ever said a word to me, but from time to time, he'd send little notes saying, "Nice headline; who wrote that?" As I gained a little confidence, I realized we didn't have to be entirely gray just because we're The Good Gray Lady. I got a little more reinforcement from him and from other editors, and even from some of the reporters.

Good. How's your desk organized?

We have six or eight copy editors, "rim people" they were called in the old jargon, and we have a slot man. Copy desks used to be shaped like horseshoes, and the person in charge sat in the middle in the slot. Now we have a bunch of computers, and our desks are all lined up in a row.

Trace a typical story down the pipe.

Okay. The reporter writes the story, and it comes into what we call "the backfield," where the assigning editors do preliminary work. Then it comes to the copy desk. The slot man..., or slot woman..., the *slotperson* assigns it to whichever of the rim editors is available.

What kind of instructions come with the story?

Nothing but copy at first. We simply pick up the story and begin editing it.

What does editing consist of?

Don, bear with me while I tell you what copy editors do and don't do.

Be my guest.

Copy editors do not have a lot of information at our fingertips. We do not know, for example, that reporters have a staggeringly difficult job.

We do not know how many p's Parsippany, New Jersey, has in it. We do not have reference works to double-check spelling, or the accents in foreign languages.

We do not have broad knowledge. We do not know Mayor Dinkins's middle initial. We do not know what irony means, and whenever we encounter it in a story, we take it out.

We do not realize that in the process of writing, a reporter with fingers flying over the keys can write "Cuomo" when he or she means "Clinton." We sit half dozing and slumping at our terminals without understanding any of those things, and the only time we sit erect is when something comes flopping onto our desk.

When we were working on paper, we'd take the story and smear paste all over it. Then we'd cut it apart and start transposing paragraphs.

Sometimes we eliminate parts of sentences. If we have time, we remove all the vowels. If we have a chance to rewrite the lead, we do that, sometimes inserting information that we know to be incorrect. After a while, we ship it on to the next editor, who does the same things. (We do this blindfolded, by the way.) We write a headline, focusing on a minor element of the story, not the news.

Then we go to the composing room, and ask the printer to paste a completely different story under the wrong jump head. On a story about a mayoral press conference, we try to be sure it gets in under a headline that has something to do with the St. Patrick's Day parade.

Boy, I never knew your job was so hard. [Laughter]

Then we realize the story is six inches too long. This gives us particular glee because we have the opportunity to cut it in a gross way. So we cut as much as we can, but we're still three inches over. So we ask the printer to take the bottom three inches back over to page one. Then we take out the lead and the byline, and place those three inches at the top of the story. Then we go to lunch.

All that before lunch. Such dedication. [Laughter]

We grouse about the reporters while we're drinking our lunch. At three o'clock in the morning, we call the reporter and ask him if he knows whether Boutros Boutros-Ghali has a hyphen in his name. So that's what we really do.

Well, that's the end of the conversation. Now I understand everything. [Laughter]

Right. You asked.

Okay. How much latitude do you have in making changes?

If a word is misspelled or an accent isn't correct or has been left out, I can correct it. If there's a hole in the story, if the story seems unbalanced or unfair, I can't fix that.

Do you send it back?

I talk to the reporter. We pretty much all talk with the reporters here. We're not insulated and isolated from them by other editors, which has been my experience at other papers. It's great to be able to talk directly to the reporters, to be able to understand what they're trying to say.

Can you change grammar without consulting?

I'm free to change grammar if I'm perfectly clear on what the writer intends to say. A dangling participle can be ambiguous, and I want to talk to the reporter about that.

Can you change quotations?

No. Quotes are considered sacred.

How about leads?

I'd only change a lead in conference with a reporter. We're lucky in this department. A lot of times, we have the reporter with us, and both of us can be looking at the screen at the same time. I try to represent..., *all* copy editors try to represent the reader. If I stumble, I assume other readers may stumble.

When you say, "looking at the screen at the same time," do you mean electronically or physically?

In many cases, literally.

That's great. After correcting and buffing, then what?

One of the most important things I do is trim. I do everything I can to trim without major damage. I can hyphenate and justify the copy the way it's going to appear in the newspaper. If I can save a whole line by eliminating a word or a widow somewhere, that's a lot less painful than taking a sentence out to save a line. Usually I'm working with a reporter here. But sometimes, the reporter isn't available, and I just have to say a prayer, grit my teeth, do what has to be done, and try not to get too much blood on the newsroom floor.

So when I've got it trimmed and buffed, I send it to the slot person, the person in charge of the desk, who originally gave it to me. He reads it, and raises questions with me, occasionally with the reporter.

Who writes subheads?

Generally the copy editor writes all the headlines and subheads. That includes what we call "blurbs," which are smaller, upper- and lowercase complete sentences set into the type of the story.

Give me an example.

On the jump page of "Clocks Are Fugitive," look at "Scurriers need big and little hands in plain view." That's a blurb. [See photo, page 217.] Elsewhere in the paper, a standard hard-news story is going to have little subheads, which are relief devices, as are the blurbs. The blurbs are also there to give the copy editors a chance to amplify the headline, to catch the underlying significance, particularly in a hard-news story.

What are subheads for?

On pages laid out early in the day, we know how long the story should be and how the legs of type are going to turn, so we're asked to break the type with subheads to relieve the reader's eye. Or maybe to tantalize the reader if we get a nice turn of phrase leading into the paragraphs that follow. It's eye relief and also a bit of a summary of what's to come.

I think of subheads as introducing sections for the reader. I write my own, even for magazines that don't publish them. Do you think of them as section markers, or just as graphic devices?

I can't normally allow myself to think of them as marking sections. The graphics dictate their placement. If I knew the story was a little short, I'd normally put a subhead in.

Do you write the jump headlines?

Yes.

So you need to know the story's going to jump.

Yes. In our department, I'll know, for example, that a story's going to start on page C-1 of the Living section, and jump to C-6. So I get a head order, a jump-head order, and probably some blurb orders. I'm going to be alerted to the fact that there are captions, and that I need to double-check them against the story.

Who writes the captions?

A picture editor writes our captions for us. Sometimes I may rewrite captions if the editing of the story turns up something that makes the caption incorrect. If the caption echoes a headline that I've written, and shouldn't echo it, then I might rewrite the caption.

Do you have the pictures and the captions in front of you when you work on the story?

Yes. We usually have a layout or a copy of the photograph.

Sounds very organized. Let's talk about headlines, subheads, blurbs, captions, all the things you write or edit. What makes them good?

A headline is probably more important these days than ever before to invite readers in, and to help them open the door into stories. I'm very lucky in being able to work in a features section, because I can be a little more invitational. I can certainly be a little more playful than someone who's writing a headline about 400 law agents in a standoff with a Texas cult. You have to get information in those headlines presented in such a way that a reader can understand it, and to telegraph the most important thing in the story.

So it has to be clear and essential, as well as inviting. What invites readers in?

If they smile when they read the headline, if they're tickled a little bit, they might want to read the story. If they see something in the headline they recognize, common phrases, not clichés necessarily, but something familiar that takes a little twist, it might provoke them into looking a little farther into the story.

Should the headline capture the whole story?

It can't. First of all, if you're lucky, you can get the most important information into the headline, if you've got space and words enough within the rules of writing headlines. Second, if you're even luckier, you can play. You can try to be clever. You can try to be attractive.

What do you mean by "if you're lucky"?

If you have patient editors who'll give you an extra five minutes (my editors are patient). If you don't have a one-column headline into which you have to cram a whole lot of information, and all of it in long words. That sort of thing.

Look at "We Are the World; We Are the Crayons." What's good about that headline?

It takes something that most of the readers of newspapers in this country today know about: "We are the world. We are the children." Suddenly at the very end, it twists, and where you expect to see "children," you see "crayons." The little article that follows is about how Crayola, in response to some requests, has tried to be more multicultural in the colors of crayons.

And that song, "We Are the World...," is multicultural.

Yes. It is.

I compared your headlines with their stories to see how many of the words of the story you use in the head. Here the only word you use is "crayons."

There's an obliqueness to almost all of these headlines. This one tries to convey a tone and some information, while at the same time having a little fillip to pique the reader, if you will.

Whom do you think of as that reader?

I have to think of myself as the reader. I'm editing and writing headlines for myself, my wife, my editors, my Allan Siegal. I think the reader is someone who can read. I can't characterize the reader otherwise.

Some *New York Times* staffers think of themselves as "elites writing for elites." Do you think that way?

No! To me, those are fighting words! I think that anyone can read the paper. The people who are writing and editing the paper are probably elite. I'd have to concede that.

I'm focusing on *"for* elites."

I thoroughly and utterly disagree with that! I think that we're writing this paper for everyone who can read, and for everyone who wants to have a grasp of the world around them. There may be many who are offended by some of the things they read in it. There may be some who are enraged by the grammatical errors that somehow slip between my fingers, or are typed in by my fingers, God forbid.

You have a New York audience, yet the paper is a national, even international newspaper. Do you keep that dual readership in mind?

Sometimes we use expressions, turns of phrase that are very specific, very parochial....

Very New-Yorkish....

They're very New York. I don't think you're going to see the word "tchotchke" in many other newspapers.

What does it mean? [Laughter]

Let me look it up before I tell you what it means, or I'm going to get it wrong. I think it's from the Yiddish, if not Yiddish itself. [Long pause] Well, it's not in my dictionary. I'm using the old one here. I'll have to get it for you. I'm embarrassed now. [Laughter]

Don't be. What do you think it means?

A little curiosity. Perhaps a little object you have some sentimental attachment to. A little bit of clutter in your household, or on your desk.

What the French call a "bibelot"?

I think so. But I may be a thousand miles off on that, so I'd really like to check it. That's the kind of word we use occasionally. It's a more New-York-specific word than it is, say, a San-Francisco-specific word, or a Houston- or Dallas-specific word.

Now tell me how you write headlines. What goes on in your head?

I'm talking about features here. I'm not talking about hard news. You don't have to sit back and scratch your head over what to put at the top of a story that talks about "Much Bosnian Aid Missed Its Target."

Exactly.

Well, sometimes I just lean back in my chair and get away from the story for a minute. I might have it on the screen; I might not. Then I just let all the things that have dropped into my personal hopper over the years go to work on the story. With luck again, a lot of reading, a fair amount of experience in writing headlines for newspapers, and particularly for *The New York Times,* a phrase suggests itself. Maybe not the phrase that actually appears in the headline, and maybe not the phrase that has anything to do with the headline as it finally appears in the paper. My headlines are, if not rewritten by others, sometimes rewritten by me at their behest. Sometimes they just don't fit the story, or they're a little askew.

But at some point, I'm scratching my head, and a phrase pops in, and I start playing with it.

Do you play with it out loud, or in your head?

In my head, mostly. I might write down six or seven phrases that suggest themselves to me on a piece of scratch paper, and let them all bounce off each other while everything in the hopper is working on them. Then I say, "Okay, I want to use this phrase, or I want to use this idea, this thought." Then I lay my hands on the computer keyboard, and I try to write the headline to the specifications I've been given.

Before you lean back, do you read the whole story?

Copy editors are asked to write early headlines for pages sometimes. But normally I don't try to write a headline until after I've finished editing the whole story. I have to lean back at that point, because I'm very much in the thick of the story. I'm very close to it, and sometimes I don't even know what it says, because I've been so close to it. I've been dotting i's and crossing t's, and doing very close work.

We call that "cooling off." So you don't think about the headline as you're editing.

Unless I see something that really grabs me, no, I don't. In fact, I try not to. Sometimes I bog down if I try too soon when I'm halfway through a story. I like to have the whole impression of the story before I write the headline.

Stories have different lengths, of course, but in general, how much time do you spend on each one?

Boy, that's a bit of a minefield.

Well, watch your feet. [Laughter]

Well, look at "Clocks Are Fugitive," a lovely essay by Betsy Wade. I might've spent an hour reading that story, and maybe asking her a question if I had to chase her down. On "We Are the World; We Are the Crayons," I might've spent ten minutes. As I read that story, I probably, for example, wanted to be sure about what we call the Reverend Dr. Martin Luther King Jr. Do we use the "Jr."? Do we use the "Reverend"? Do we use the "Dr."? So I had to do some checking. Sometimes I get a little confused over the brand name here. Is it "Crayon" or "Crayola"? I never can quite remember. It *is* "Crayola," so that's the one that gets uppercased. I might've called the 800-number near the end of the story to make sure someone's fingers didn't slip when it was typed into the system.

Oh, bless you, and all copy editors like you!

I can't say I do that every time, especially in stories that have a vast number of telephone numbers. But if we have a local number, I like to call it, because if you're talking about something bad that has happened, or a product that's being discussed, some poor person is going to get an awful lot of telephone calls who does not want them.

This particular headline probably suggested itself pretty quickly. I might sit for another ten minutes on that headline before it comes out of nowhere. These things come out of nowhere. They really do.

Is the minimum time ten minutes?

Oh, I can't imagine I'd spend any less than ten minutes on a story of even five or six paragraphs. I have spent an entire workday on a story; seldom longer than that. It depends on what the story is about and how long it is, how involved it is, how dense it is (I'm not going to venture too far into that!), how well written it is. And, how far away and accessible the reporter is.

I have to say that you're very lucky having all that time, and so are your reporters.

·I have to say that I deeply appreciate the luxury of time I have at *The New York Times,* particularly in departments, not just my own, where we're working in advance on stories, and it's clear that our editors want us to take the time we need to take. At the same time, we need to close pages on time, and sometimes you just have to cut things short.

You seem to have lots of people to help you. You're not doing things like layout, for instance.

No. I'm not doing layout at the same time that I'm editing stories. I'm not making up pages. I'm usually not formatting copy.

You don't type in font codes and stuff like that.

Normally, the rim editors don't. As production editor, I would do that. It's a nice change of pace.

250

How did you come up with "Clocks Are Fugitive: Will Father Time Now Carry a Watch?"

This story was published on New Year's Day, as you can see. Betsy Wade, who has a lovely style, is complaining about the loss of clocks in public places. So the first thing that suggested itself to me was *"tempus fugit"* (time flies), and that didn't quite work, so I used a portion of it in "Clocks Are *Fugit*ive."

"Father Time" comes from the date, I assume, but Father Time doesn't appear in the story.

Right. I'll reach for phrases..., for turns of phrase. I'll reach for words that aren't in the story, and that, in some cases, aren't even glanced at in the story.

Talk about the blurb: "Scurriers need big and little hands in plain view."

In hard-news stories or in analytical news stories, blurbs are intended to capture the underlying significance of the article. The headline is supposed to give the reader the main fact or facts, and then the blurb underlines the next most important point. It can't read out of the headline; you can't have "he" in a blurb, referring to the name of someone in the headline. Blurbs are also graphic devices, intended to break up type. They're intended to lighten The Good Gray Lady.

How did you come up with "scurriers"?

Someone is scurrying in the story. You're going around town, and you need to know what time it is. I don't think that's in the story either.

That wonderful word "scurriers" captures New York life on the streets.

I can't remember, frankly, whether I had the layout in front of me, but it didn't hurt that we

had this big photo from 47th and Broadway.
You get the sense of the hurly-burly hubbub of
the city in this picture on the jump page.

**You turn rapper in "Wanna Rap? Let It Rip:
All You Do Is Add the Lip."**

Well, I'm not good at rap. My experience with
street life is limited to crossing Times Square
on the way to work, but I wanted to try it. I
wanted to make sounds in the headline, sounds
that one might imagine made by rappers.

Did you speak this one out loud?

I probably mouthed it, or whispered it to myself. I think headlines are better seen than
heard. They're going to have to work by being
seen, so I really don't say them out loud very
much. I had to check the meter and the rhyme,
so I suspect I said it to myself. Some of these
headlines have a kind of meter to them.

Most of them do.

I don't think most readers notice that, but I
think it's something we have in common, a
sense of rhythm, a sense of meter. You can be
jarred by a headline that might say something
very playful or clever, but doesn't quite scan.

It'll jerk the reader with the wrong rhythm.

And it might make the reader turn the page
and say, "To hell with it." That's quite the opposite of what I'm trying to do.

**Speaking as a writer, I regard your headline as
my first sentence, and I'd like it to match *my*
rhythm. Or not sound out of rhythm, that's the
way to put it.**

Right.

Earlier you gave me an ironic list imitating how reporters..., well, *some* reporters..., *too many* reporters think about copy editors....

Of course, copy editors don't know what the word "ironic" means.... [Laughter]

Of course. Now, what do copy editors want from reporters?

Sympathy. In some papers, because of the dayness of reporting and the nightness of copy editing, there are artificial barriers between reporters and copy editors in terms of schedule, in terms of distance, in terms of time, in terms of different professional necessities.

Actually, I think we can't expect anything from reporters that we haven't tried to explain to them. We ought to say to the reporter, "I didn't mean to screw up your lead. I did it totally by accident. I was editing your story too fast. I'm sorry." If there's anything I'd like from reporters, it would be a sense that I could go to them and say, "This is why I did what I did," and maybe be met halfway with an understanding that I'm here not to hurt, but to help.

Right. Do you find most reporters receptive to that?

I do. I've worked in this department for ten years, and the reporters have brushed up against me and bounced off me enough to know me, to know if I'm truly what I claim to be: one who wants to help and not hurt.

Do they ever thank you?

Yes. I almost get a catch in my voice. [Pause] That's about as high as I can get. This must be the hardest thing for a reporter to say: "You saved me. Thanks a lot."

I don't find it hard to say that. I'm a writer, and I depend on copy editors. I want squads of them between me and my reader. And when they save my ass (and they do!), I say, "Thank you for saving my ass." And I'm not ashamed of it at all.

Well, you must be a very confident writer, because it's the most confident reporters who can come to me and say thanks.

Confidence comes from knowing you've got teammates who'll help you get it right. Teammates like you.

Jules Ned Crabb

Finalist, Headline Writing

Jules Ned Crabb has worked at the *Tulsa* (Okla.) *World,* the *Miami News, The Miami Herald,* and the *New York Daily News.* He joined *The Wall Street Journal* 17 years ago, and now edits the Letters to the Editor column.

Crabb wrote his headline from this sentence in the middle of a letter: "Perpetual buck-passing, like mutual back-scratching, runs rampant not because it is so tempting but because it is so easy." He preserves the author's play on "buck/back" but turns the nouns into active verbs: "Pass the Buck, Scratch the Back."

Letters to the editor:
Pass the buck, scratch the back

Rep. Dick Armey (R., Texas), in his review of Martin Anderson's book *Impostors in the Temple* ("Socialism on Campus," *Leisure & Arts,* Aug. 19), is right on the money about what ails academia. (Academia even sounds like a disease.) Yes, it is fraught with intellectual arrogance, mutual back-scratching, escalating incompetence and exploitation of subordinates. But most of the maladies he cites are epidemic outside academia as well. What else can be expected from interlocking boards of directors, thick layers of middle management, judges with lifetime appointments and perennially unopposed members of Congress? The "divorce of power from responsibility" is not the exclusive province of professors, much less the "essence of socialism." It is found in all sorts of large institutions, where the real problem is not so much the evasion as the diffusion of responsibility. Perpetual buck-passing, like mutual back-scratching, runs rampant not because it is so tempting but because it is so easy.

Academics aren't the only impostors. CEOs, bureaucrats, talk-show "experts," economic prognosticators, "technical" analysts and baseball managers may not get tenure, but they have an uncanny ability to stick around. Mr. Armey complains that professors don't make their living according to the quality of their ideas, unlike those in the private sector (but here compare GM with 3M). One reason he "left academe," he says, "is that professors aren't forced to live with the consequences of their ideas." In fact, most of their ideas don't have consequences. Unfortunately, Rep. Armey and his colleagues, even if they are forced to live with the consequences of their ideas, aren't forced to pay for them.

—Kent Bach, San Francisco State University

Gene Weingarten

Finalist, Headline Writing

Gene Weingarten managed to avoid graduating from college. We're not sure what he did during his Nieman Fellowship at Harvard, but he assures us that he did meet "the grueling academic requirement of remaining alive for the entire year." Before that, he edited *Tropic,* the Sunday magazine of *The Miami Herald,* maintaining a proper level of looniness in Dave Barry's columns. Now he edits the Sunday Style section of *The Washington Post.*

His runner-up headline, "The First Lady or The Tiger," plays on the traditional dilemma, while the straighter jump head, "Defining First Ladyship," captures the essence of the story.

The First Lady or The Tiger

NOVEMBER 18, 1992

By Martha Sherrill

Hillary Clinton arrives in town today still in the process of figuring out how to be an impeccable incarnation of Midwestern virtue, the modern symbol of American womanhood, the soft embodiment of sacred motherhood and wifedom, the pride of the Seven Sisters, the new icon of progressive legal causes, the inspirational emblem of volunteerism, and *lovable* at the same time.

For two weeks now, she has been The Sphinx of Little Rock, contemplating her new role, flipping the hypotheticals around in her capable mind, pondering the sensitive politics of her new position. Yesterday her husband made clear that she already has a key position in the transition—but helping Bill settle on a secretary of state may be the easy part. "She realizes how important her decisions are," says her press secretary, Lisa Caputo, "and wants to take time making them."

You can almost hear the cheering from the sidelines. Women all over—Republicans, Democrats, feminists and anti-feminists—have endless opinions about what she should be. Bill Clinton, after all, is just another president, but his wife has already come to signify much more. There's talk of cosmic consequences, gender solidarity and generational transformations. Is this a Hillary Cult in formation? There's a needy feeling, too, that nobody has yet figured out exactly how to be a wife and a mother and a professional—easily—and that maybe Hillary Clinton will figure it out for everybody. Her gain is our gain, her loss would be our loss—that sort of thing. Nobody wants to see her mess it up. But how on earth should she do it?

"I don't think she has to have a specific job," says Nan Keohane, president of Wellesley College. "The one thing about law is that it's a flexible profession. She can take on projects and assignments which flex her muscles as a lawyer, but which is not seen as a conflict of interest."

Even though there's a 1967 law prohibiting a relative of the president from serving in a post under his jurisdiction, Anna Perez, press secretary to Barbara Bush, sees nothing wrong with Bill Clinton eventually giving his wife a job.

"If she wants to make policy, there's certainly no reason for her not to," says Perez. "It's clear she is eminently qualified for a job in an administration, and if the *only* thing keeping her from a job is because she's married to the president, then that's grossly unfair."

"When people get appointments because of their relatives, it usually disturbs people," says Phyllis Schlafly, lawyer and antiabortion activist. "Frankly, I don't think that's a problem. I'm more concerned about what kind of advice she gives."

Heather Foley runs the office of her husband, House Speaker Tom Foley. From her office in the Old Executive Office Building, Marilyn Quayle was in husband Dan's inner loop and affected policy—with little controversy. Nancy Reagan scheduled her husband's presidential activities—and her influence didn't seem as outrageous as the fact that it was guided by astrology. When Rosalynn Carter sat in on Cabinet meetings, people laughed that she was a busy-body wife.

Behind the scenes advice-giving works for some, it would seem, but not others. How does Hillary Clinton navigate these dark, mysterious waters? "She can be anything she wants to be as long as she's likable," says Sally Quinn, Washington journalist and author. "Haven't you noticed that people who are really well liked can do anything they want? It's almost a marketing thing....

"And if she has an influence," says Quinn, "then she should be upfront about it. Her role, as she defines it, should be clear to everybody. It does seem to me, though, that she'd have an easier time—and avoid an enormous number of problems—if she has a job. If she doesn't, any involvement she has could make her seem like a meddling wife."

Liked? Loved? "I hope she'll continue to be friendly but not tame," says Clarissa Pinkola Estes, Jungian analyst and author of *Women Who Run With the Wolves.*

"I hope Hillary Clinton will be willing to give us the advantage of what she knows and does well," says Mary Dunn, president of Smith College. "And I hope she won't be overly intimidated by people who insist that the role of First Lady be domestic."

"There should be a new title for what she does," says Patricia Ireland, president of the National Organization for Women. "'First Lady' seems like a very dated term."

First Woman? Ireland admits that she was concerned when it appeared that Hillary changed her image to suit voters—first changing her last name from Rodham to Clinton, then banishing the headband when people made fun of it, then the cookie baking, then the silence. "But it's always hard to argue with success," says Ireland. "The Clinton campaign was clearly sensitive to the Republican efforts to make her look like a witch...like The Bad Woman."

All these mythic classifiers: The Good Woman, The Bad Woman, The Witch. In the world of self-reflection and women and Jung and transformation, authors suddenly have found a new archetype. After chewing on the meaning of Madonna, the debate may be turning to the meaning of Hillary. Who will she be?

Savvy behind-the-scenes lobbyist or ceremonial blond fixture? Protector of children and defender of women's rights, or, the president's wife who carries his speeches in her suit pockets? What blend of being, what potpourri of talents will Hillary Clinton choose to exercise?

"She's the same beautiful woman—whether she's lawyering, mothering or lobbying the president," says Marianne Williamson, lecturer and best-selling author of *Return to Love*. "The most important issue has less to do with what Hillary Clinton does, and more to do with us," she continues. "Can we become a nation which criticizes less and honors more? Can we tear a woman down less, be threatened by her less, and support her more? That's what *The Hillary Issue* has really been about: not whether she is too strong, but whether or not the American psyche is ready to handle a strong woman without punishing her."

Camille Paglia believes the so-called "Hillary Issue" is entirely up to Hillary—not the American psyche, which Paglia believes is something more fixed than alterable. According to Paglia, the controversial author of *Sexual Personae,* Hillary Clinton's success and popularity will be determined by her image—as televised.

"During his *60 Minutes* interview, Bill Clinton appeared to be an overgrown mouse on his wife's leash," Paglia says. "This issue remains. People keep asking, *Why was Mrs. Clinton at the dinner with the Democratic leaders?* Well, the explanation goes that she's more knowledgeable than he is about some things. So, the big question mark in everybody's head is now: *Who is the real president? Hillary or Bill?* I'm personally thrilled that he's so respectful of women, but we never want a man who is a leader to bow to his wife's dictates. It's very tricky. We have elected him and not her."

We didn't elect James Baker either.

"A wife is in the bedroom and James Baker is not," Paglia replies. "Sex is a very important thing. My theory of sex is that the woman is dominant. The man seems to be on top, but he isn't.... The important thing is that we don't want to sense that she's calling the shots."

Then she adds: "But I should also tell you —I have a great sense of exhilaration."

A sense of exhilaration, and a sense of history. "She can be someone who will leave big footprints behind," says Estes. "I have never in my entire life felt so proud when I realized that she would be our First Lady—that we wouldn't have one who simply did the gardening circuit, hugging babies and visiting orphanages."

"I felt so good the day after the election," says San Francisco writer Diane Middlebrook, "that I sent her a copy of my biography of Anne Sexton [whom Middlebrook portrays as a groundbreaking feminist]. I believe that the generational shift that Hillary Clinton represents is incredibly important to this country... We're all waiting to hear from her."

A sense of expectation too. "It's so unfair," says Kate Michelman, director of the National Abortion Rights Action League. "One of the things we have to be careful about is putting expectations on Hillary Clinton that are impossible to achieve. It's almost The Supermom Syndrome—she's supposed to be able to do everything. We don't want to burden our First Lady with expectations that can't be met...but I must say, it's hard not to. It's so exciting!"

Dorothy Rodham is a bit worried about expectations too. Four months ago, when she was asked at the Democratic convention what kind of First Lady she thought her daughter would become, she said, "I see her as a combination of Eleanor Roosevelt and Jackie Onassis." Now, although proud of her daughter's potential as role model, Rodham is circumspect.

"I just hope people don't forget," she says, "that Hillary's a human being."

Observations on headline writing

While we were sorting through the entries in this part of the ASNE contest, Deborah Howell announced that her all-time-favorite headline was written by Bob Byrne for the *Minneapolis Star* back in 1971, for a story about the burial of a famous American poet:

They're Going
To Stash
Ogden Nash.

That was greeted with a few smiles and a couple of laughs, but also by a wince or two and a number of groans. Which reminded us that not everyone agrees about what constitutes a terrific headline, and that one person's idea of wit can be another person's idea of a bad joke.

This is the first year that ASNE has given a prize for headline writing, and Judy Clabes and I, who made the first stab at sorting through the entries, set the criteria as we went along. We started with the definition that James Naughton of *The Philadelphia Inquirer* used in the letter that accompanied his paper's entry. "A headline should be accurate, literate, and appealing," he wrote, and should "capture the sense of the writer's work." We added the standard of Mary Hadar of *The Washington Post* that a good headline should lure readers into a story, that it should "sing siren songs."

We then decided that a good headline should do all of this without undercutting the reporter in the process, without telegraphing a lead, ruining a kicker, or stripping away any element of suspense the writer was trying to build.

Not all the entries met these criteria. In truth, some reminded us of Wolcott Gibb's lament during his time as an editor of *The New Yorker* that "Our writers are full of clichés, just as old barns are full of bats." Taken together, they suggested that America in 1992 was a place where rain fell on many parades, where innumerable people would shop 'til they dropped, where recycling plans were getting trashed from all corners, where fowl acts were committed against many birds, and where everything and anything seemed to have gone with the wind.

But as the winning entry shows, there were wonderful headlines as well: lively and provocative yet carefully done, siren songs that were at once alluring and precise. And there were other gems in the mix. Mary Smith from The *Mesa* (Ariz.) *Tribune* wrote this headline for a story saying that the earth probably wouldn't be destroyed by a passing asteroid after all: "If You Can Read This, Asteroid Wasn't Too Close." Beth Witrogen McLeod of the San Francisco *Examiner* topped a story about the CBS television show *Fish Police* with "Serving Up Fish Shticks." And Jules Ned Crabb of *The Wall Street Journal* pulled readers into a letter to the editor that claimed health benefits from wine drinking with "Bacchus Health Plan."

With these entries as the standard, the writing awards committee is waiting anxiously to see what headline the Poynter Institute editor will put at the top of this report.

Anthony Marro, Editor
Newsday

[*Editor's Note: I'm stuck with the header "Observations on headline writing," so I offer this footer:*

    ASNE Eds
    Praise Copy Eds
    For Super Heads.]

Writing short

BY DON FRY

"It's not that our long stories are too long. Our short stories are too long."
—Carl Sessions Stepp

Top editors thunder in memos, demanding shorter writing in their newspapers. Their staffs resist, even print longer stories.

Six factors keep news stories long: status based on length, defensive writing and editing, blaming readers, failure to define "short," assuming reporters know how to write short, and resistance to rampant *USA Today*-ism.

BIG STORIES, BIG STARS

Journalists equate length with status. Cub reporters begin with obits and cop briefs, and dream of investigative series. Big stories, big play, big star. Little story, B-4, no byline.

Juries weigh entries instead of reading them, judging by the way they award prizes to mega-projects and blockbuster stories. Around Pulitzer time, mailboxes bulge with fat reprints.

The ASNE Writing Committee tackled the problem head-on, with "Short Writing" as a category for their 1991 Distinguished Writing Awards. The jurors gave the prize to six sidebars accompanying an eight-page special report and a big story on Desmond Tutu. Old habits die long.

ALL THE BUTT THAT'S FIT TO COVER

Defensive writing and editing clog stories. Consider this scenario: The city editor passes

---

[*Editor's Note: Shorter (and less political) versions of this piece appeared in ASNE Bulletin, Sept. 1992, pp. 18-20, and Coaches Corner, March 1992, pg. 2.*]

on the boss's dictum to write shorter, then chews out a reporter because a competitor's story has details he "missed." The next day, all the cityside reporters write longer, putting everything they know into their stories to cover themselves. The city editor fumes that her reporters "just don't get it."

Editors add weasel phrases to avoid anything in their sections that might offend anyone higher up. One copy editor added "a famous cartoon character" after the name Mickey Mouse to fend off screaming the next day by the news editor. Editors believe that sprinkling "alleged" all over stories keeps lawyers out.

BLAMING READERS

Falling circulation started the pleas for shorter writing. Editors blame readers for not buying the paper, labeling them "a visual generation," uninterested in news, not interested in reading at all. Some editors instruct writers to pitch stories at a fifth-grade reading level.

Meanwhile, readers yearn for something worth reading. The paper responds with stories that begin like this:

The City Council Thursday by a 3-4 vote rescinded its prior roll-back of the 3.74% increase in the UDAG set-aside.

We clutter the pages with paper-of-record government news, and wonder why people don't read it. They don't read it because it's boring, with all the risk and juice mashed out by editors seeking safety at all costs.

Instead of providing readers with interesting stories written in interesting ways on interesting subjects, editors fantasize that people who don't like to read just might read shorter stories. Even if badly written, at least they end sooner.

HOW LONG IS "SHORT"?

I never met an editor outside *USA Today* who could define "short writing." Journalists think it means reporters turning in shorter copy, and editors cutting more.

I asked six civilians what they considered short writing; all six said short stories don't jump. Joann Byrd of *The Washington Post* speculates that readers define "short" as "easy to deal with."

Journalists define "short" in column inches, five to 12, depending on the context. In the *1991 APME Writing and Editing Report* (pp. 7-8), Ben Sheroan of the Owensboro (Ky.) *Messenger-Inquirer* describes his paper's helpful scheme of story lengths:

Brief: Five inches or less, no jumping

Compact: Under 12 inches, "minimum of storytelling," no jumps

Substantive: "Merits more exploration," 12-20 inches, jumps

Detailed: Over 20 inches, jumps

Roundup: Bulleted summaries, limited jumps. Notice the tie of length and treatment, a major step toward precision over mere column inches.

Let's distinguish between short *forms* and short *technique*. We might accept Owensboro's "Brief" and "Compact" as short forms. Short technique means writing concisely, or "tight."

Writing short means choosing short forms and writing tightly.

TRAINING SHORT

Top editors think their reporters know how to write short, but perversely won't. But few reporters know how, because nobody taught them. Did anyone in your schooling ever mention writing short, much less teach you how?

USA Today manages to get shorter writing. The key word here is "manage." Short writing requires rethinking training, attitudes, and habits.

Peter Prichard quotes an internal training document that stresses *USA Today*'s difference from other newspapers: the paper assumes that its "readers are upscale, well-informed, and looking for a supplement to—not a replacement for—their regular newspaper" (*MacPaper,* p. 187).

USA Today designed a new, shorter writing style to fit that reader. They learned how to produce short stories, and retrained their staffs, despite considerable resistance. That training continues, because without it, old habits lengthen stories.

Some *USA Today* quirks are easy to copy: just tell the graphics department to tilt and color the weather map. But short writing does not happen at the wave of a memo.

FIGHTING *USA TODAY*-ISM

Many journalists resist pressure from higher-ups to imitate *USA Today* in any way, because they see it as the rosy path to thin reporting, thin writing, fat graphics, jingoism, and treating readers like simpletons. Tom French, a voluminous newsfeatures writer at the *St. Petersburg Times,* says, "*USA Today* has learned to take the writing out of writing."

Many journalists see short writing as the first step toward turning their newspaper into *USA Today,* or worse. So they ignore the blizzard of memos from on high, and ward off *USA Today*-ism by not writing short.

I admire *USA Today*'s defining what they wanted and training people to produce it. But I do not endorse their assumptions or their style, both inappropriate for general newspapers.

So why write short? Short writing opens space in a tight newshole for longer, explanatory writing. Readers want quick reads on smaller subjects, meaning subjects that do not require lots of explanation. And short writing has punch, which makes it stick in the readers' emotions and memory.

SHORTENING YOUR NEWSROOM

To get short writing into our newspapers, we need to stop blaming our readers. When newspapers publish interesting stories about interesting people, readers respond with surprise and delight. "Interesting" does not mean goody-goody prose or celebrities. Jim Nicholson of the

Philadelphia Daily News has built a huge readership writing obits about relentlessly ordinary people: an iceman, a Tastycake retiree, a guy who gave parties.

Second, we can redesign our reward systems to encourage short writing. We should start with bylining short stories. Ask a reporter to write short now, and you ask her to give up her precious byline.

The newsroom can sponsor a contest for the best short-form story. Short-form beats might gain high status by putting stars and salary increases on them. The paper can create anchored spaces for short forms, such as the Charleston (W.Va.) *Daily Mail*'s 150-word "Backtalk" slot at the bottom of the editorial stack. Editors can reward good short writing by praising the writer who wrote it loudly and in public.

Third, editors and reporters have to abandon defensive habits. They might agree to ban gratuitous "alleged" and "allegedly" and "according to police sources," even "police said" from the paper.

Editors should talk with reporters about what's *in* the story rather than what *isn't,* preferably before the reporter writes; then they collaborate early rather than fight later. Above all, journalists need to start writing and editing for readers, and not for each other.

Editors have to take responsibility for teaching their reporters how to think short and write short. Here's how.

HOW TO WRITE SHORT

Mark Twain apologized, "I'm sorry to write you a long letter. I didn't have time for a short one." Writing short requires more assurance, planning, revision, and time.

First, *negotiate length, and design the story to that length.* Writers who negotiate length immediately after finishing the reporting will write to that length..., well, maybe 10% over. With no length in mind, writers write long, because they like the stuff they've collected and want to display it.

Notice the verb "negotiate." Only the reporter knows how complex the issues are; only the editor knows the overall space. The two collaborate on a length after a brief consultation. The writer keeps his side of the bargain by planning the story to fit that length, and the editor jockeys to keep that much space available. They renegotiate as conditions change.

Second, *work from a written plan.* Writing in short space, especially in short time, requires discipline. The writer selects only those parts, facts, and details needed to tell the story, and then plans their order. Keep plans short, just labels for the parts, like this:

Lead: Men's Movement
1. Tom-toms
2. Bly in loincloth
3. Women snicker
Kicker: "Unnatural rhythm."

Without a written plan, good stuff in the notebook tempts the writer to stray. The planless writer gets carried away with tomtomming. Writers can change the plan if they think of a better one.

Third, simple leads work best for short writing, so *lead with the essence of the story.* To find that essence, ask: "What's the story about?" Draft a one-sentence answer, and revise it later. Fussed-over leads end up full of qualifiers.

Jump into the action, avoiding introductions and set-ups. To find "the action" in the blur of detail, ask: "What happened?" Then ask: "Yeah, but what *happened*?"

Then get out fast. Wilbur Landrey, the *St. Petersburg Times* star foreign correspondent, tells how he explains so much in short columns: "I start as late in the action as I can, and stop as soon as I can."

Writers rev up with set-ups and throat-clearing at the top. Such scaffolding may help the writer, but slows down the reader. So don't write it in the first place, or, if you must, whack it out later.

Taylor Buckley coached half a decade of *USA Today* writers to shortness. He advises, *"Make your point early."* A story needs a point, one dominant idea that holds all the details together. The sooner readers know the point, the easier readers can handle complex explanation.

Quotations complicate reading, so *use just a few quotations, those that capture essences and require less apparatus.*

Every quote requires baggage:
- Attribution, often including title and organization
- Punctuation: minimum , " ,"; but sometimes , " ," , " ."
- Two voice changes: writer to speaker, back to writer.

Few sources speak prose, so quotations seldom have the clarity that prose demands. We have to add contexting, and sometimes a paragraph telling what the speaker really meant.

We demand three sources in the notebook for any assertion, so reporters cram all three into the story in quote form.

Timid editors cling to the mistaken notion that attribution prevents lawsuits, so they add it everywhere, one attribution per sentence. Excessive attribution clogs the flow, so, outside of quotes, *attribute only when absolutely necessary.*

Make every sentence add to the readers' knowledge and understanding. Put one idea in each sentence. During revision, examine each sentence to see if the readers need that idea.

Limit transitions. Revise them out, or don't write them in the first place. One good phrase or word makes a better transition than a sentence or two, and we should ask if readers needs a transition at all. But writers should not hesitate to start a sentence with "but" to mark a transition, despite their teachers.

Some material works better in non-narrative form; *push such information into graphics, pictures, sidebars, blurbs, at-a-glance boxes, bulleted lists, cutlines, and headlines.* Any description of things moving in complicated space, such as a collision in an intersection, makes for long, hard reading; but a diagram simplifies explanation.

Copy editors now write blurbs, at-a-glance boxes, cutlines, and headlines, although I can foresee a time when reporters will. But smart writers suggest material for those forms to copy editors, and smart copy editors appreciate such extra effort and help. Copy editors and reporters can confer early, and divvy up the information.

Journalists use verbs appropriate for packing a suitcase to describe short writing: "stuff," "cram," "squeeze," "mash." Writers stuff sentences so full that readers can't read them, like this:

Even while the number of reportable serious crimes exploded after 1945, the courts, understandably more impressed by the horrors of Nazi Germany than by what was going on in the streets of Detroit and Chicago, spelled out that the Constitution gives a person accused of a non-Federal offense the right to have a lawyer, just as those accused of Federal offenses have.

I didn't make that up. A large grey metropolitan daily printed it.

Write simple sentences. Start with the subject. Put the verb next. Don't stick things inside things. Keep related things together. One sentence, one idea. It's economy, stupid.

Taylor Buckley adds: *"Propel the story with punctuation."* Our Stylebook hates punctuation, on the theory that it slows down sentences. So we get sentences like this: "On the courts below the birds 30 elderly people are playing shuffleboard."

Punctuation speeds readers up by showing where phrases and clauses begin and end. Think of punctuation as road signs on a well-marked freeway, as units of meaning that cost only one space.

Writers short on space delete people in favor of data, which makes the stories less human. Storytelling requires people acting, preferably action that readers can visualize. So *describe gestures and actions to reveal character.* Head-to-toe description does not help readers, but little gestures make characters seem real, like this: Mayor Cate adjusts his starched cuffs and laments, "Nobody seems to work here after 5 p.m." Short writing uses narrative touches rather than narration.

The Inverted Pyramid wastes space by devaluing the bottom half of the story and assuming that unseen beings in dark places will whack off endings.

Every story needs an ending. *Use a kicker to cement the story in the readers' memory.* Readers remember best whatever they read last, and the kicker provides the glue to make things stick in their heads.

Finally, writers need to *submit copy so perfect that editors won't lengthen it.* Perfect finish and exact, agreed-to length calm the editors' anxieties and help keep their fingers off the copy.

Reporters should write with such assurance that editors and readers know they know what they're talking about. (Of course, it helps if the reporters *do* know what they're talking about.) Writers should chat with editors and copy editors to ease their qualms.

NEW ATTITUDES AND OLD TRICKS

These new attitudes and old techniques would improve all newswriting. We might coax our readers back with interesting, concise stories about human beings, regardless of length.

Annual bibliography

BY LUZ NELIDA MIRANDA

This selected bibliography of recent books and periodical articles focuses on the art and craft of writing for newspapers. Also included are items on reporting, composition, coaching, editing, and the teaching of writing.

BOOKS

Times Style: The St. Petersburg Times Guide to Style, Policy and Good Writing. St. Petersburg, FL: Times Publishing Company, 1992.

Clark, Roy Peter, and Don Fry. *Coaching Writers: The Essential Guide for Editors and Reporters.* New York: St. Martin's Press, 1992.

Digregorio, Charlotte. *You Can Be a Columnist: Writing & Selling Your Way to Prestige.* Portland, OR: Civetta Press, 1993.

Ehrlich, Henry. *Writing Effective Speeches.* New York: Paragon House, 1992.

Fischer, Heinz Dietrich. *Medicine, Media, and Morality: Pulitzer Prize-Winning Writings on Health-Related Topics.* Malabar, FL: Krieger, 1992.

Garrison, Bruce. *Advanced Reporting: Skills for the Professional.* Hillsdale, NJ: Erlbaum Associates, 1992.

—. *Professional News Reporting.* Hillsdale, NJ: Erlbaum Associates, 1992.

Hickey, Dona J. *Developing a Written Voice.* Mountain View, CA: Mayfield Publishing Company, 1992.

Jerome, John. *The Writing Trade: A Year in the Life.* New York: Viking, 1992.

Kessler, Lauren, and McDonald Duncan. *The Search. Information Gathering for the Mass Media.* Belmont, CA: Wadsworth Publishing Company, 1992.

Killenberg, George M. *Public Affairs Reporting: Covering the News in the Information Age.* New York: St. Martin's Press, 1992.

Murray, Donald Morison. *Writing for Your Readers: Notes on the Writer's Craft from The Boston Globe.* Old Saybrook, CT: Globe Pequot Press, 1992.

Noble, William. *The 28 Biggest Writing Blunders (And How to Avoid Them).* Cincinnati, OH: Writer's Digest Books, 1992.

Parsigian, Elise K. *Mass Media Writing.* Hillsdale, NJ: Erlbaum Associates, 1992.

Plotnik, Arthur. *Honk If You're a Writer: Unabashed Advice, Undiluted Experience, and Unadulterated Inspiration for Writers and Writers-To-Be.* New York: Simon & Schuster, 1992.

Rubens, Philip. *Science and Technical Writing: A Manual of Style.* New York: Holt, 1992.

Shuman, R. Baird. *Resources for Writers.* Englewood Cliffs, NJ: Salem Press, 1992.

Ward, Jean, and Kathleen A. Hansen. *Search Strategies in Mass Communication.* New York: Longman Publishing Group, 1993.

Weinberg, Steve. *Telling the Untold Story: How Investigative Reporters Are Changing the Craft of Biography.* Columbia, MO: University of Missouri Press, 1992.

Whittemore, Katharine. *Voices in Black & White: Writings on Race in America from Harper's Magazine.* New York: Franklin Square Press, 1992.

Wingate, Anne. *Scene of the Crime: A Writer's Guide to Crime-Scene Investigations.* Cincinnati, OH: F&W Publications, 1992.

ARTICLES

Aucoin, James. "The New Investigative Journalism." *Writer's Digest* 73.3 (Mar. 1993): 22-27.

Bain, George. "Drowning in a Sea of Clichés (news reporting)." *Maclean's* 105 (21 Sept. 1992): 52.

Bartel, Pauline. "Quick and Clean Interviewing." *Writer's Digest* 72.11 (Nov. 1992): 36-37.

Bernay, Anne, and Paul Hemphill. "Journalists as Fiction Writers." *Nieman Reports* 46.1 (Mar. 1992): 71-80.

Boo, Katherine. "The New Writers' Bloc." *Washington Monthly* 24.11 (Nov. 1992): 36-41.

Boston, Bruce O. "Portraying People with Disabilities: Toward a New Vocabulary." *The Editorial Eye* 15.11 (Nov. 1992): 1 + .

Braddock, Clayton. "The Value and Power of Metaphors for Future Professional Writers." *Journalism Educator* 47.1 (Mar. 1992): 80-84.

Burnside, Sharon. "12 Steps to Better Reporting." *The Editor* (Oct. 1992): 18-20.

Cannon, Keith. "Notes from the Front Lines: What Journalism Students Need." *Editor & Publisher* 124.34 (22 Aug. 1992): 44.

Carroll, Jon. "Stop Me If You've Heard This One." *San Francisco Chronicle* 7 Apr. 1992, E: 12.

Cela, Camilo Jose. "Spain's Nobel Prize Winner Offers 12 Commandments of Journalism." *Editor & Publisher* 125.41 (10 Oct. 1992): 54.

Davis, Ron. "The Pause that Refreshes—and Informs." *ASNE Bulletin* 740 (Apr. 1992): 39.

—. "Subbing for 'Said'." *Masthead* 44.4 (Dec. 1992): 27.

Davison, Peter. "To Edit A Life." *The Atlantic Monthly* (Oct. 1992): 92+.

Dozier, Steve. "Re-Evaluation of Traditional Writing Techniques Overdue." *Editor & Publisher* 125.2 (11 Jan. 1992): 44.

Dwyer, Edward J. "Using a Journalism Model for Teaching Essay Writing." *Journal of Reading* 36.3 (Nov. 1992): 226-7.

Friend, Cecilia. "Computerized Records and Newspapers." *Editor & Publisher* 125.52 (26 Dec. 1992): 9-10.

Fry, Don. "'Writing Short' Means Writing for Readers, Not for Each Other." *ASNE Bulletin* 743 (Sept. 1992): 18-20.

—. "You Can Coach Short Writing." *The Coaches' Corner* 7.1 (Mar. 1992): 2.

Gibson, Martin L. Red. "Don't Let Tenses Jerk You Around." *The Coaches' Corner* 7.1 (Mar. 1992): 8.

Gillies, Patrica. "Making Sure It All Adds Up." *The Editor* (July 1992): 22.

—. "Verb 'Said' Bores Writers, not Readers."
The Editor (Feb. 1992): 11.

—. "When Farmers Pray for Soggy Fields: The Comma Is More Than a Device To Let Readers Catch Their Breath." *The Editor* (Aug. 1992): 20.

—. "Word Misuse Takes Toll on Language."
The Editor (June 1992): 22-23.

Gow, Joe. "Writing Rock Journalism: An Interview with Charles M. Young." *Popular Music & Society* 16.2 (June 1992): 67-74.

Halverson, Roy. "Electronic Data Bases Transform Writing and Editing Courses." *Journalism Educator* 47.2 (June 1992): 85-88.

Harrigan, Jane. "Finding the Story." *Writer's Digest* 72.4 (Apr. 1992): 36-39.

Harris, Arthur S. Jr. "Writing the Newspaper Travel Article." *Writer* 105.2 (Feb. 1992): 21-23.

Hart, Jack. "The Art of Storytelling." *The Coaches' Corner* 7.1 (Mar. 1992): 1.

—. "Cutting to the Quick." *Editor & Publisher* 125.46 (14 Nov. 1992): 24.

—. "Our Passive Voices." *Editor & Publisher* 125.41 (10 Oct. 1992): 28.

—. "Writer's Workshop: Building on Basics."
Editor & Publisher 125.12 (21 Mar. 1992): 4+.

—. "Writing Clinic." *Quill* 80.1 (Jan. 1992): 40,45.

Kirkhorn, Michael J. "Journalism's Guilty Secret (imagination in journalism)." *Nieman*

Reports 46.2 (June 1992): 36-41.

LaRocque, Paula. "Clarity is the Top Priority." *APME News* 194 (Feb. 1992): 11.

—. "Fad Usages Erode the Language." *APME News* 197 (Aug. 1992): 15.

—. "Find the Hidden Facts in a Backed-in Lead." *APME News* 196 (June 1992): 18.

—. "Quotations: The Spice of Write." *Quill* (June 1992): 40-41.

—. "A Steady Diet of Cliches Has Made Papers Hard to Digest." *APME News* 195 (Apr. 1992): 13.

—. "Tongue Tied." *Quill* (Apr. 1992): 39-41.

Leonard, Teresa. "Databases in the Newsroom: Computer- Assisted Reporting." *Online* 16.3 (May 1992): 62-65.

Levoy, Gregg. "Finding Your Voice As A Writer." *Byline* 148 (Sept. 1992): 10-11.

McKeen, William, and Glen L. Bleske. "Coaching Editors to Coach Writers with Team Teaching Approach." *Journalism Educator* (June 1992): 81-84.

McManus, Kevin. "If You Absolutely, Positively Have to Talk to Real People." *ASNE Bulletin* (Nov. 1992): 18-19.

Miller, John. "How to Edit Without Being a Jerk." *The Editor* (Oct. 1992): 21-22.

Mueller, Douglas. "Good Leads, Bad Leads." *Editors Only* 10.3 (Mar. 1992): 6.

—. "More Ways to Achieve Clarity." *Editors Only* (Oct. 1992): 5 + .

—. "Tips on Overcoming Writer's Block." *Editors Only* 10.5 (May 1992): 6-7.

Simon, David. "The Reporter I: Cops, Killers and Crispy Critters." *Media Studies Journal* 6.1 (Dec. 1992): 30-43.

Snyder, Dianne. "When Writers Have Trouble Getting Started." *The Editorial Eye* 15.12 (Dec. 1992): 1-3.

Spikol, Art. "Doity Woids-Warning: This Column Contains Words Some Readers May Find Offensive." *Writer's Digest* 72.11 (Nov. 1992): 60-63.